W9-AWK-109

SCHOLASTIC

TEACHING READING THROUGH DIFFERENTIATED INSTRUCTION WITH LEVELED GRAPHIC ORGANIZERS

Nancy L. Witherell and Mary C. McMackin

NEW YORK · TORONTO · LONDON · AUCKLAND · SYDNEY
MEXICO CITY · NEW DELHI · HONG KONG · BUENOS AIRES

Teaching *Resources*

*To our parents Anthony and Bertha Kopcych
and Tom and Helen Carew, with love.*

*We would like to thank all the classroom teachers who took the time
to try out the activities in this book. Their feedback, insights, and
encouragement were invaluable.*

Susan Bergstrand, grade 4

Gayle Bradbury, grade 8

Helen Collis, grade 6

Jaime Daley-Reid, grade 6

Grace Nagle, grades 7 and 8

Kristina Pontes, Reading Specialist

Dr. Sandra Robinson, Literacy Coordinator

Debbie Soares, grade 4

Rayna Tulysewski, grade 4

Ronnie Zusman, grades 3 and 4

*We would like to send a special thank you to our editor, Sarah Longhi
of Scholastic Professional Books, for all her help and guidance
throughout this process. We could not end these acknowledgments
without thanking "the cheerleaders," our husbands and children.*

Cover design by Maria Lilja

Interior design by Sydney Wright

ISBN: 0-439-79554-0

Contents

Introduction

What Is Differentiated Instruction?

Differentiated instruction is not only a way of teaching, but an educational philosophy. It is the desire to meet the needs of all students, regardless of where they fall on the skills spectrum. Carol Ann Tomlinson, in *The Differentiated Classroom: Responding to the Needs of All Learners* (1999), gives clear explanations and insights into understanding differentiated instruction, detailing a new approach for designing lessons, helping educators understand how to obtain optimal success for all learners.

How Do Teachers Differentiate Instruction?

When you differentiate instruction, you choose to modify either the content, process, or product for individual learners while teaching all students the same skill or concept. This modification may make the task simpler for the students who need more support or more difficult for students who need to be challenged—it all depends on individual students and their needs.

When you differentiate instruction through product, as in this book of leveled activity pages, you assign students material or information on an appropriate instructional level. For example, if your intended outcome is to have students identify the perspective of characters on a particular event or situation, you would match students with the leveled response that they can complete successfully—and in the end, all students would come away from the experience understanding the concept of character perspective.

Differentiation also requires flexibility. Once a student successfully completes the lowest-complexity task, he or she may be assigned the next level so the learner is continually being challenged. What is important to keep in mind is that, regardless of the level, the lesson's objective does not change. This consistency allows students to build skills and confidence for success at higher-level activities.

About This Book

Teaching Reading Through Differentiated Instruction With Leveled Graphic Organizers gives teachers practical approaches for differentiating reading instruction by what students produce— the organizers and activity pages that follow. In these tiered response activities, the expected outcome always remains the same. For example, the skill outcome for all Story Maps activities is for students

to recall information from the story and label story elements, including characters, setting, problem, and solution.

The three activity pages gradually increase in difficulty. The introductory level asks students to come up with the title, main characters, setting, problem, and solution. The intermediate level requires students to give more details in the description of the setting and to list all attempts to solve the problem. Finally, in the challenging level, students must categorize characters as major or minor, state effects of the setting, and describe both primary and secondary problems, attempts to accomplish goals, and the solution. Each level is purposely designed to require more of the reader than the last, so that each assignment is increasingly challenging.

How to Use This Book

The diverse group of grades 4–8 teachers who tested these organizers all took different approaches; they used the graphic organizers for leveled responses, as an avenue for scaffolding, and for individual projects. How you decide to use these graphic organizers will depend on your students' needs, your academic goals, and your teaching style. Keep in mind that by modeling the target skill prior to assigning the graphic organizers, you help prepare students to better understand and complete the activity. You'll find teaching tips under the Model Lesson section of each chapter and further teaching tips under the description of each organizer.

❀ Leveled Responses

Some teachers modeled the introductory level organizer in a large-group mini-lesson and then assigned the three organizers according to the needs of each student. Assessment was instantaneous. Teachers recognized immediately when a task was too easy or too difficult, and had the students try a different level or made a note to assign them the more appropriate level when they reviewed that skill.

How the leveled responses were assigned depended on individual teaching styles. For example, some teachers approached the assignments in the same way they assigned leveled books in guided reading; they explained to their students that every reader is different and requires a different challenge. If students were uncomfortable—or too comfortable—with the activity, the teacher would encourage them to try a different level. These teachers emphasized individual challenge and flexibility. They made sure no student was "trapped" on a particular level.

❀ Scaffolding for Success

Grace Nagle, a seventh-grade teacher, used the graphic organizers for scaffolding students' learning. When she began to use tiered responses for character analysis (page 38), her students noticed the different assignments and questioned why they couldn't do those activities they hadn't been assigned. A master teacher, Grace explained they were welcome to try a different response. Some students deepened their exploration of a character by completing the character analysis organizers at all three levels for the same character. Although some of their answers remained the same at each level, their confidence and knowledge grew as they completed each organizer. Eventually, as students become more adept at the focused skill, the lower-level tasks no longer need to be offered. In this way, a group of students might move through each level to master the target skill.

❀ Individual Projects

Teachers also used these graphic organizers as part of their end-of-book project or as independent reading assignments. Some teachers selected a particular set of organizers for the final project, and a few required that students complete more than one level for a given skill. When students were reading individual choices, teachers selected graphic organizers that were compatible with the book each student was reading and the skills that each student needed help with.

No matter how the teachers decided to use the graphic organizers, one point became clear: *There must be a match between the graphic organizer and the book.* If the book contains many time and place descriptions, you might select the Setting or Details activities. If the book's theme is important to today's lifestyles, the Personal Connections activities may be most appropriate.

Final Thoughts

There is no doubt that meeting the needs of all students does take time, effort, and commitment. The tiered activities in this book are designed to help simplify this task. Each of our graphic organizers has been used successfully and enthusiastically in classrooms. The lessons are written in first person to provide you with a clear model of how skills can be presented to students, and each chapter begins with an explanation of how to use each activity or graphic organizer to offer the appropriate challenge for every student.

Personal Connections

Skill: *Establish relevant connections between the text and one's schema*

About Personal Connections

Personal connections are links that readers make between the information presented in the text and their own experiences and other relevant background knowledge (schema). In the graphic organizers for this chapter, the phrase "my own experiences" refers to what has happened personally to the reader, while "other connections" refers to stories, events, or facts that the reader has not experienced directly, but has heard or read about.

> A *schema* is a well-organized, mental network of a reader's prior experiences and background knowledge. This network helps readers connect new ideas to what already exists in their memories.

Why Is This Skill Important?

Making personal connections helps readers relate to events, characters, themes, and other story elements, which deepens their comprehension and investment in the text.

GETTING STARTED

Model Lesson: Making personal connections with *Island of the Blue Dolphins* by Scott O'Dell (Dell, 1960)

* **Read aloud from an engaging, short passage.** I select a paragraph about otters from *Island of the Blue Dolphins* with which I feel comfortable making connections both through direct experiences and background knowledge:

> The sea otter, when it is swimming, looks like a seal, but is really very different. It has a shorter nose than a seal, small webbed feet instead of flippers, and fur that is thicker and much more beautiful. It is also different in other ways. The otter likes to lie on its back in the kelp beds, floating up and down to the motion of the waves, sunning itself or sleeping. They are the most playful animals in the sea. It was these creatures that the Aleuts hunted for their pelts. (page 15)

* **Draw connections between the text and direct experiences.** I explain that when I read I stay engaged and learn more by making connections between what the author writes and my own experiences. I think out loud, "O'Dell's description of the way the sea otters look and behave reminds me of a time when I visited an aquarium and watched sea otters at play." I go on to describe how I, like the author, am keyed into the differences between sea otters and

seals and share with students what I know about how they look and how they act and communicate. I explain that I can connect the information in the book directly to experiences I've had.

✴ **Draw connections between the text and background knowledge.** I point out that the last line about the otters being hunted for their pelts reminds me of a newspaper article I read recently about how minks are being raised and then killed for their fur. This makes me wonder: Is this similar to what is happening to the otters? Did the Aleuts hunt the otter as a way of life? Was the killing necessary or only for profit? I'm making connections to other sources rather than to my direct experiences. I explain that making connections gets me more involved with what I'm reading, and when I make connections I enjoy my reading, understand it better, and want to learn more.

✴ **Help students make personal connections on their own.** I invite students to pick a section of a book or article we're reading as a class that they feel they can connect with. I ask individual students

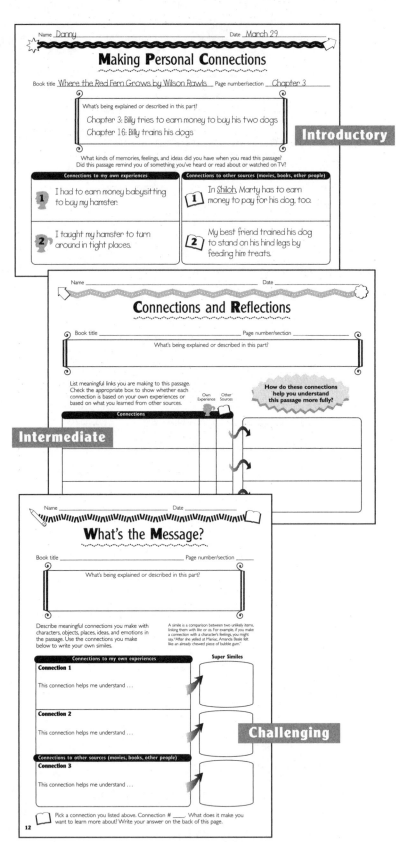

to share a connection they've made and then ask the rest of the class whether that connection links the reader's direct experience to the passage (like my visit to the aquarium), or whether it links experiences that go beyond the reader's direct experience (like my reading about the mink being raised for their fur).

＊ **When students can make personal connections and distinguish between direct experiences and information they have from other sources, match them with the appropriate tiered activities.**

USING TIERED ACTIVITIES

Readers will:

❀ Briefly summarize the passage. [All]

❀ Make connections to their own experiences and background knowledge. [All]

❀ Reflect on how these connections help them to understand the text. [Intermediate and Challenging]

❀ Create a simile that shows the connection between a character, place, or thing in the book and a dissimilar, but appropriate, person, place, or thing. [Challenging]

Graphic Organizers:

Introductory Level: Making Personal Connections (page 10)

Tip: If students are having problems getting an idea from "other sources," let them interview another student to get relevant information. This student becomes the other source.

Intermediate Level: Connections and Reflections (page 11)

Challenging Level: What's the Message? (page 12)

Tip: Make sure students understand what a simile is before completing the activity. I point out that a simile is a type of *connection* authors make between ideas. (See chapter on figurative language for more information on similes.)

Books Worth Using:
Yellow Bird and Me by Joyce Hansen (Clarion Books, 1986)

The Midnight Horse by Sid Fleischman (William Morrow & Co., 1990)

Encounter by Jane Yolen (Harcourt, Brace & Co., 1992) *Picture book*

Name _____ Date _____

Making Personal Connections

Book title _____ Page number/section _____

What's being explained or described in this part?

What kinds of memories, feelings, and ideas did you have when you read this passage? Did this passage remind you of something you've heard or read about or watched on TV?

Connections to other sources (movies, books, other people)

Connections to my own experiences

Name _____

Date _____

Connections and Reflections

Book title _____

Page number/section _____

What's being explained or described in this part?

List meaningful links you are making to this passage.
Check the appropriate box to show whether each
connection is based on your own experiences or
based on what you learned from other sources.

Own
Experience

Other
Sources

How do these connections
help you understand
this passage more fully?

Connections

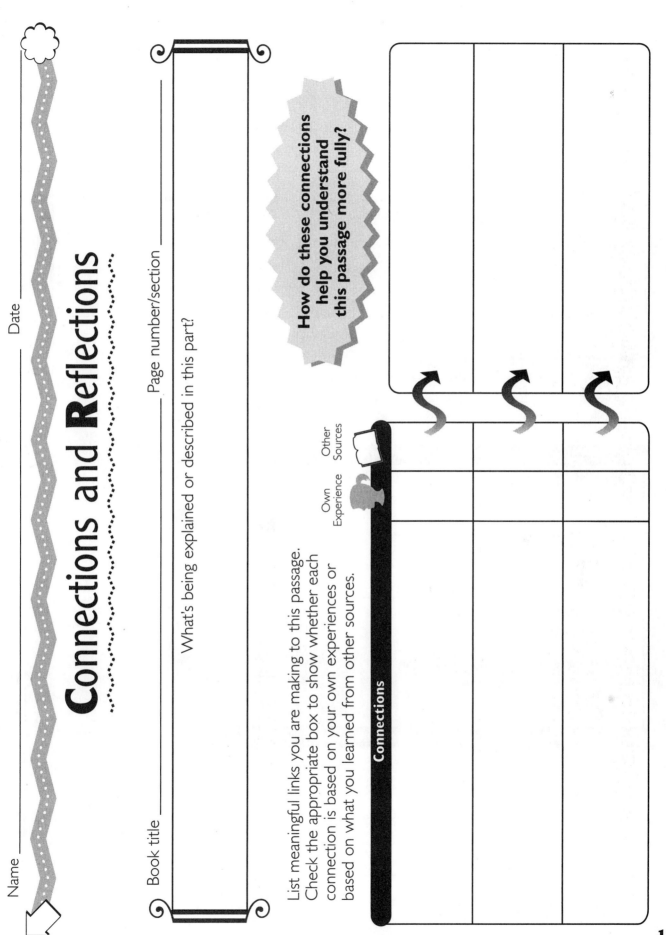

11

Name _____ Date _____

What's the Message?

Book title _____ Page number/section _____

What's being explained or described in this part?

Describe meaningful connections you make with characters, objects, places, ideas, and emotions in the passage. Use the connections you make below to write your own similes.

A simile is a comparison between two unlikely items, linking them with *like* or *as*. For example, if you make a connection with a character's feelings, you might say, "After she yelled at Maniac, Amanda Beale felt like an already chewed piece of bubble gum."

Super Similes

Connections to my own experiences
Connection 1
This connection helps me understand . . .
Connection 2
This connection helps me understand . . .

Connections to other sources (movies, books, other people)
Connection 3
This connection helps me understand . . .

 Pick a connection you listed above. Connection # _____. What does it make you want to learn more about? Write your answer on the back of this page.

Think Abouts

Skill: *Use strategies to self-monitor reading comprehension.*

About Think Abouts

Good readers use a variety of monitoring strategies to comprehend texts. These strategies include, but are not limited to, prediction, explanation, elaboration, visualization, asking questions, and drawing conclusions. Less accomplished readers may not realize that these strategies exist, while others may be aware of them but may not be able to apply them. Teachers and students may use think abouts as a way to share the thought processes they use to construct meaning from print. Students can "see" exactly what strategies to use while reading.

Why Is This Skill Important?

When students can explain their thinking, we gain a clearer picture of what goes on in their minds as they comprehend a story. Teachers can assess whether the student is misinterpreting or confusing issues in the story as they do think abouts. More important, this also helps students see their own confusion as they discuss their thoughts with others.

GETTING STARTED

Model Lesson: Using think-about strategies with *Roll of Thunder, Hear My Cry* by Mildred D. Taylor (Bantam Books, 1976)

* **Select a short passage to model several think-about strategies you use to better understand the text.** In these introductory paragraphs, Taylor describes a scene in which children are walking to school. The youngest is about to make them late. She writes:

> "Little Man, would you come on? You keep it up and you're gonna make us late."
>
> My youngest brother paid no attention to me. Grasping more firmly his newspaper-wrapped notebook and his tin-can lunch of cornbread and oil sausages, he continued to concentrate on the dusty road. He lagged several feet behind my other brothers, Stacey and Christopher-John, and me, attempting to keep the rusty Mississippi dust from swelling with each step and drifting back upon his shiny black shoes and the cuffs of his corduroy pants by lifting each foot high before setting it gently down again. (page 1)

* **Think aloud about the strategies you used and note the places in the passage where you stopped to reflect.** Although there are a number of strategies that can be used to construct meaning, I use this passage to focus on prediction, personal connections, and asking questions.

First, I *predict*, saying, "I wonder if the child telling this story is afraid that she (or he) will be late for school again. The

author gave me some pieces of important information that led me to this prediction. She let me know that Little Man was holding a notebook and lunch box, and that all the children were headed for the same place. It must be morning (before lunch), so I think they are all on their way to school. When good readers make a prediction, they often want to go back and check the evidence once they've read on to confirm or change their original prediction." I encourage students to put a stick-on note by the passage and record their predictions.

I can also use this passage to *connect what I'm reading to an experience I've had* by saying, "I know exactly how the narrator of this story feels. I used to have a friend, Tessa, who lived near me when I was a young girl. No matter where we were going, Tessa made us late. I bet the narrator is getting frustrated with Little Man, just as I used to get irritated with Tessa. When I make connections like that to my memories and experiences, I feel more involved in and care a lot more about what I'm reading."

Finally, I *ask questions* while reading by saying "I wonder why Little Man is so dressed up? Are the other children dressed up, too? None of them seems to be worried about staying clean." I ask students how questioning what's going on can help them as readers. They realize that a question can help a reader get focused to find important information and clear up confusion—in this case,

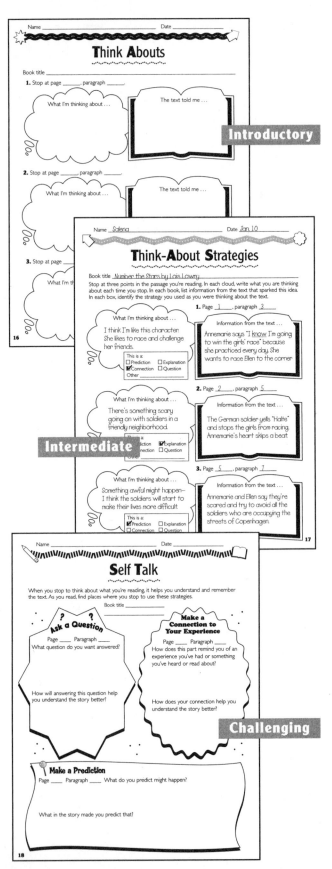

about the personalities of the characters and their behavior in this setting.

* **Model different types of think-about strategies frequently and provide lots of opportunities for students to practice these strategies.*** Encourage students to be aware of the strategies they are using by recording their thoughts on stick-on notes or in a journal and frequently discussing strategies with you and with their peers.

* **When students can show their thinking about their reading by making predictions, drawing personal connections, explaining to clarify, and asking questions, match them with the appropriate tiered activities.**

USING TIERED ACTIVITIES

Readers will:

❀ Identify what they are thinking about the text during reading and show evidence from the text to support this thinking. [All]

❀ Predict, make connections, or ask questions while reading. [All]

❀ Name the strategy they used when thinking about the text. [Intermediate]

❀ Reflect on how the strategy helped them better understand the story. [Challenging]

Graphic Organizers:

Introductory Level: Think Abouts (page 16)

Tip: Help students show where they might stop and think by assigning a page number and paragraph at which to respond. Students can compare their responses in small groups. Guide students toward the intermediate level by having them name the type of strategy they used.

Intermediate Level: Think-About Strategies (page 17)

Tip: In their books or passages, students might mark "thinking spots" with different colored stick-on notes to show what kind of think-about strategy they used at a particular point.

Challenging Level: Self Talk (page 18)

Tip: The questions in each shape are designed to help students think critically about how and why they are using each strategy.

. . . .

Books Worth Using:
Homesick, My Own Story by Jean Fritz (GP Putnam, 1982)

Out of the Dust by Karen Hesse (Scholastic,1997)

Train to Somewhere by Eve Bunting (Clarion Books, 1996) *Picture book*

* Note: You may need to spend time exploring each of these strategies separately. Roger Farr (http://www.rogerfarr.com), the creator of "think-alongs," stresses modeling each component. Students should be encouraged to support their thinking with evidence from the text.

Name _____ Date _____

Think Abouts

Book title _____

1. Stop at page _____, paragraph _____.

What I'm thinking about . . .

The text told me . . .

2. Stop at page _____, paragraph _____.

What I'm thinking about . . .

The text told me . . .

3. Stop at page _____, paragraph _____.

What I'm thinking about . . .

The text told me . . .

Think-About Strategies

Book title _____

Stop at three points in the passage you're reading. In each cloud, write what you are thinking about each time you stop. In each book, list information from the text that sparked this idea. In each box, identify the strategy you used as you were thinking about the text.

1. Page _____, paragraph _____

What I'm thinking about . . .

Information from the text . . .

This is a:
☐ Prediction   ☐ Explanation
☐ Connection   ☐ Question
Other _____

2. Page _____, paragraph _____

What I'm thinking about . . .

Information from the text . . .

This is a:
☐ Prediction   ☐ Explanation
☐ Connection   ☐ Question
Other _____

3. Page _____, paragraph _____

What I'm thinking about . . .

Information from the text . . .

This is a:
☐ Prediction   ☐ Explanation
☐ Connection   ☐ Question
Other _____

Name _____   Date _____

Self Talk

When you stop to think about what you're reading, it helps you understand and remember the text. As you read, find places where you stop to use these strategies.

Book title _____

_____

? ? Ask a Question

Page _____ Paragraph _____
What question do you want answered?

How will answering this question help you understand the story better?

Make a Connection to Your Experience

Page _____ Paragraph _____
How does this part remind you of an experience you've had or something you've heard or read about?

How does your connection help you understand the story better?

Make a Prediction

Page _____ Paragraph _____ What do you predict might happen?

What in the story made you predict that?

Visualization

Skill: *Create a mental picture of events, characters, and settings while reading to clarify elements of the book.*

About Visualization

Visualization enables readers to interact with the text by making a picture of what is happening as they read. As readers become more adept at visualizing, they use images to infer, interpret, and recall the text.

Why Is This Skill Important?

When students can create mental pictures of their reading experience, they tap into background knowledge and personal experiences, building a strong reference bank for better understanding as they continue to read.

GETTING STARTED

Model Lesson: Visualizing a scene in *The Friendship* by Mildred D. Taylor (Dial Books, 1987)

* **Choose a passage that invites students to picture the action, characters, and/or setting.** I use the short chapter book *The Friendship* to show students how I picture a scene. Taylor's book portrays the lives of young blacks in 1933 and provides images and situations of a not-distant segregated past. In the book, a white storekeeper berates and upsets Little Man, a

six-year-old black boy, for having hands "so dirty that seeds could be planted" on him. Little Man defends himself, saying, "They ain't dirty. They clean." Then a white customer says, "Best chop them hands off, Dew. They that filthy!" (page 14) Little Man's siblings try to comfort him. Taylor writes: "But after a few moments he did a strange thing. He reached down and placed his hand flat to the dirt. He looked at his hand, looked at the dirt, then drew back again." (page 21)

* **Talk students through picturing the scene by "making a movie" in their minds.** I guide students with cues such as: "Close your eyes. Now see the children walking into the old-fashioned store. Picture the counter and the candy jars. What else do you see? hear? feel? Now see them leaving the store. Watch Little Man comparing his hands to the dirt. What do you see? hear? feel?" The author emphasizes that Little Man was terribly upset by the racist words and actions of the white storekeeper. I assess whether or not my students can "see" Little Man's fright, hurt, and confusion, as they infer what he cannot articulate.

✳ **Once students are comfortable with guided imagery, and they are able to describe what they "see" as they read, match the appropriate tiered activity to each student.**

USING TIERED ACTIVITIES

Readers will:

❋ Sketch their mental image of a scene and write an accompanying explanation. [All]

❋ Interact with the text through their interpretation of a story scene. [All]

❋ Use a graphic organizer with five senses to help visualize details. [Introductory]

❋ Use ideas from the graphic organizer and the picture to summarize the scene. [Introductory]

❋ Visualize and predict by drawing what will happen next. [Intermediate]

❋ Use drawings of consecutive story scenes as a rehearsal for summary writing. [Challenging]

Graphic Organizers:

Introductory Level: Scene Sketcher (page 22)

Tip: Students may not be able to complete the entire organizer as their reading may not contain descriptions that feature every one of the senses.

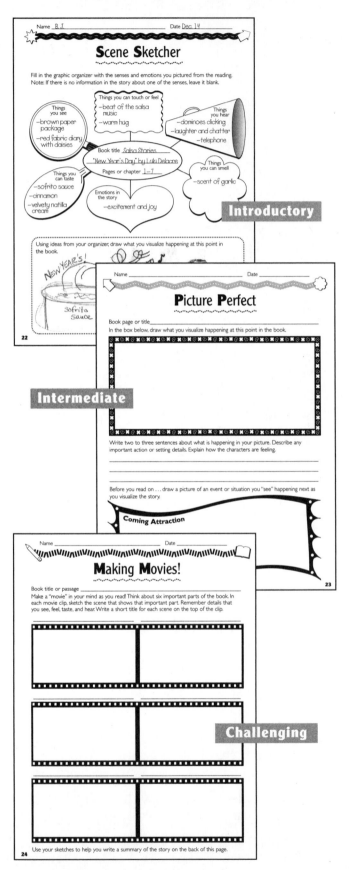

Intermediate Level: Picture Perfect (page 23)

Tip: The banner at the bottom of the page asks students to make a visual prediction. Have students working with this organizer select a point at which they've just stopped in their book to make a true prediction.

Challenging Level: Making Movies! (page 24)

Books Worth Using:

Joey Moses by Susan Duncan (Storytellers, Inc., 1997)

Park's Quest by Katherine Paterson (Puffin Books, 1988)

Nettie's Trip South by Ann Warren Turner (Macmillan Publishing Co., 1987) *Picture book*

Name _____ Date _____

Scene Sketcher

Fill in the graphic organizer with the senses and emotions you pictured from the reading. Note: If there is no information in the story about one of the senses, leave it blank.

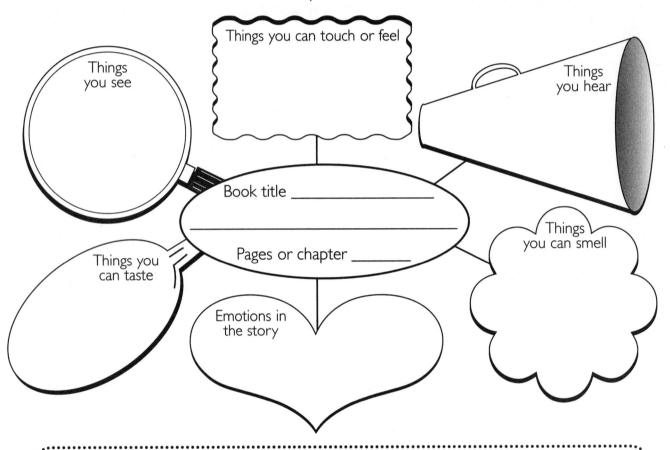

Using ideas from your organizer, draw what you visualize happening at this point in the book.

Name _____ Date _____

Picture **P**erfect

Book page or title_____

In the box below, draw what you visualize happening at this point in the book.

Write two to three sentences about what is happening in your picture. Describe any important action or setting details. Explain how the characters are feeling.

_____

_____

_____

Before you read on . . . draw a picture of an event or situation you "see" happening next as you visualize the story.

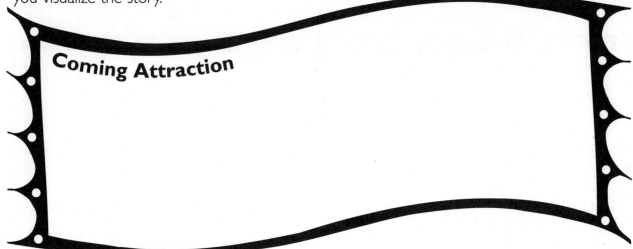

Coming Attraction

Making Movies!

Book title or passage _____

Make a "movie" in your mind as you read! Think about six important parts of the book. In each movie clip, sketch the scene that shows that important part. Remember details that you see, feel, taste, and hear. Write a short title for each scene on the top of the clip.

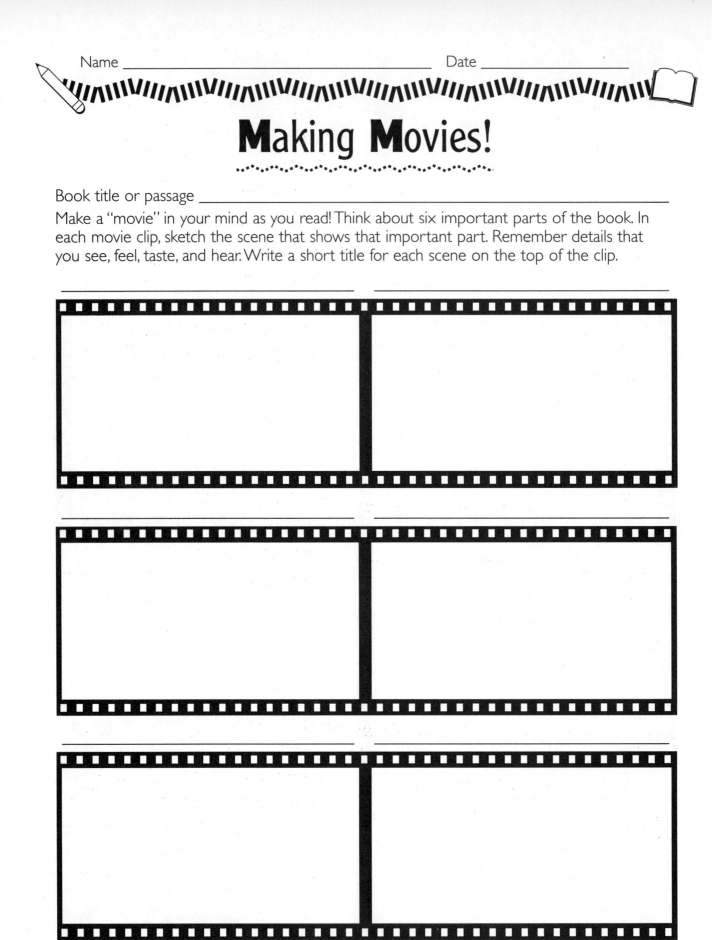

Use your sketches to help you write a summary of the story on the back of this page.

Predictions

Skill: *Use information presented in the text and prior knowledge or experiences to infer the outcome of future story events.*

About Predictions

Making predictions requires readers to infer. Because writers do not reveal explicitly everything they want readers to know, it is up to the reader to combine prior knowledge with information from the text in order to fill in these gaps and determine future events or actions. The ease of predicting depends on the amount of relevant information provided by the text, the reader's background knowledge and personal experiences, and the reader's ability to combine this information.

Why Is This Skill Important?

Making predictions keeps readers actively involved in the unfolding story. As readers make predictions, they constantly evaluate information, develop hypotheses, and then confirm or reject those hypotheses.

GETTING STARTED

Model Lesson: Making predictions with *Sarah, Plain and Tall* by Patricia MacLachlan (Harper & Row, 1985)

* **Select a passage or short chapter book and have the class agree upon a stopping point.** I choose to have students read the first two chapters of *Sarah, Plain and Tall*. In Chapter 1, MacLachlan describes how Caleb misses his mother, who died the day after he was born. Now, as a young boy, he wants to keep her memory alive by learning the words of songs she used to sing. Caleb's Papa suggests that perhaps Sarah Elisabeth Wheaton, the woman from Maine who has responded to his ad for a wife, knows the forgotten verses. The chapter ends with Caleb's sister, Anna, asking Papa to find out if Sarah sings. In Chapter 2 we see letters that Caleb, Anna, Papa, and Sarah send to each other. Caleb cherishes Sarah's letters, rereading them over and over. In her last letter, Sarah says that she'll come to visit them for a month, but she's hesitant to move so far from the ocean. She wants to see how it would be to live in a rural community out West before making a commitment. The letter (and the chapter) concludes with: "Tell them I sing . . ." (unpaged)

* **Pose a question that will prompt students to make a prediction.** After students read these first two short chapters, I ask, "How do you think Caleb might feel when Sarah comes to visit?"

25

* **Help students make inferences from the text and their own experiences to back up that prediction.** I explain that the author has given us clues that can lead us to predict that Caleb may be nervous and excited when Sarah comes to visit (for instance, he asks many questions about Sarah before she arrives). I ask students how they would feel if a very important guest were coming to stay with them. Students predict that Caleb might do something funny because he's so nervous. I point out that they've used MacLachlan's clues about the hopes and expectations Caleb has for Sarah and their own experiences to make a prediction about Caleb's future feelings and actions. Invariably students want to read on to check the accuracy of their predictions. In fact, just before Sarah arrives, Caleb is so nervous, he asks, "Is my face clean? . . . Can my face be too clean?"

* **Encourage students to write down predictions in a journal or on stick-on notes that they can attach to pages in the book where they've made those predictions.** Having them keep a record helps you keep track of their thinking and makes the predictions easy to check and either confirm or reject.

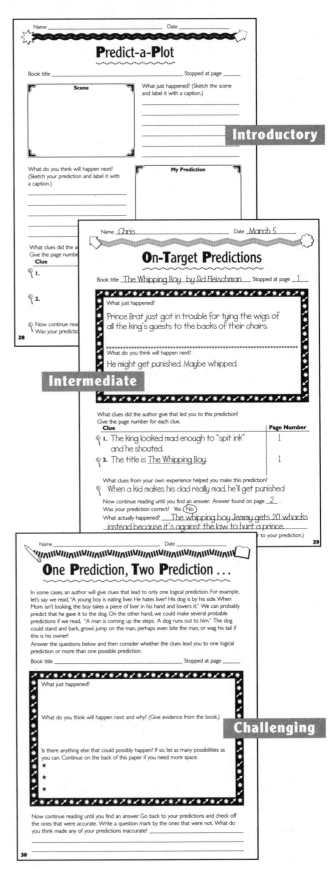

✳ **Point out that the more information the students have and the more related experiences they can apply to the situation, the more accurate their predictions will be.** As students become more advanced with this skill, they will learn to distinguish between *divergent* predictions (based on the clues, there can be multiple logical predictions) and *convergent* predictions (based on the clues, there can be only one logical prediction).

✳ **Once your students can combine information in the text with their background knowledge and experiences to make predictions, introduce them to the appropriate tiered activities.**

USING TIERED ACTIVITIES

Readers will:

❀ Make and justify their predictions with clues from the book. [All]

❀ Make explicit connections to their prior knowledge. [All]

❀ Check the prediction for accuracy. [All]

❀ Explain how the prediction might have been different from what actually happened. [Intermediate]

❀ Explain why the prediction might have been off target. [Challenging]

❀ Identify their predictions as divergent or convergent. [Challenging]

Graphic Organizers:

Introductory Level: Predict-a-Plot (page 28)

Tip: Make sure students are familiar with making personal connections to life experiences before they complete this organizer.

Intermediate Level: On-Target Predictions (page 29)

Challenging Level: One Prediction, Two Prediction . . . (page 30)

Books Worth Using:

Sounder by William Armstrong (Harper Trophy, 1972)

A Day No Pigs Would Die by Robert Newton Peck (Laurel Leaf, 1977)

River Friendly, River Wild by Jane Kurtz (Simon & Schuster, 2000) *Picture book*

Name _____ Date _____

Predict-a-**P**lot

Book title _____ Stopped at page _____

Scene

What just happened? (Sketch the scene and label it with a caption.)

_____
_____
_____
_____
_____
_____

What do you think will happen next? (Sketch your prediction and label it with a caption.)

_____
_____
_____
_____
_____

My Prediction

What clues did the author give that led you to this prediction?
Give the page number for each clue.

Clue	Page Number
1.	
2.	

Now continue reading until you find an answer. Answer found on page _____ .
Was your prediction correct? Yes No

Name _____   Date _____

On-Target Predictions

Book title _____ Stopped at page _____

What just happened?

✽✽✽
What do you think will happen next?

What clues did the author give that led you to this prediction?
Give the page number for each clue.

Clue	Page Number
1.	
2.	

What clues from your own experience helped you make this prediction?

Now continue reading until you find an answer. Answer found on page _____ .
Was your prediction correct?   Yes   No
What actually happened? _____

_____

(On the back of this page, explain how this is different from or similar to your prediction.)

One Prediction, Two Prediction . . .

In some cases, an author will give clues that lead to only one logical prediction. For example, let's say we read, "A young boy is eating liver. He hates liver! His dog is by his side. When Mom isn't looking, the boy takes a piece of liver in his hand and lowers it." We can probably predict that he gave it to the dog. On the other hand, we could make several probable predictions if we read, "A man is coming up the steps. A dog runs out to him." The dog could stand and bark, growl, jump on the man, perhaps even bite the man, or wag his tail if this is his owner!

Answer the questions below and then consider whether the clues lead you to one logical prediction or more than one possible prediction.

Book title _____ Stopped at page _____

What just happened?

What do you think will happen next and why? (Give evidence from the book.)

Is there anything else that could possibly happen? If so, list as many possibilities as you can. Continue on the back of this paper if you need more space.

★

★

★

Now continue reading until you find an answer. Go back to your predictions and check off the ones that were accurate. Write a question mark by the ones that were not. What do you think made any of your predictions inaccurate? _____

_____

_____

Story Maps

Skill: *Recall information from the story and label story elements, including characters, setting, problem, and solution.*

About Story Maps

Making a story map allows students to identify and organize the key elements in a story: characters, setting, problem, and solution. By filling in information about each of these elements in a map, students begin to see how one aspect of the story influences another. Story maps can be assigned for complicated book chapters or for an entire book.

Why Is This Skill Important?

Students gain a deeper understanding of a story when they recognize the effects story elements have on one another. Story mapping also helps students summarize.

GETTING STARTED

Model Lesson: Story mapping with *Fudge-a-mania* by Judy Blume (Dutton, 1990)

* **Lead a simple review of story elements.** By fourth grade, most students are familiar with the basic story map and can identify the key elements of a story with relative ease. I use these simple explanations as reminders:

  * **Main characters:** the people in the story who experience the big problem

  * **Setting:** where and when the story takes place
  * **Problem:** the main issue that needs to be solved
  * **Goal:** what the characters decide they need to do to solve the problem
  * **Solution:** the way the problem actually gets resolved

* **Find a short chapter (or short book) that includes all of these elements.** I use Chapter 5 of *Fudge-a-mania*. This chapter is an easy, relaxing read, yet it serves as a complete story on its own. In this chapter, three children, Pete, Fudge, and Sheila, are searching in strange, new surroundings for a lost parrot, Uncle Feather.

* **Model how to locate, organize, and discuss the elements.** As the class works together to identify each story element, I record students' responses on an overhead of the Map It! story map. The major characters in this chapter are Mrs. A, Pete, Sheila, Fudge, and Uncle Feather. The story problem is that the parrot is missing; the goal is to find the bird. The characters make numerous attempts to find Uncle Feather by shutting windows and looking around the house, forming their "search and

rescue team," looking up at trees in the new neighborhood, and asking their new neighbors if they've seen Uncle Feather. As students explain how the children tried to solve the problem, I point out that the attempts help move the plot along and show us whether the characters are achieving their goals. We then identify the story's solution: Uncle Feather has found his own way back to his cage, and it seems he had never left the house.

✱ **Discuss how particular elements work together in the story.** We discuss how this story could have taken place in a number of settings because the actual setting doesn't have a huge impact on the plot. However, the fact that Fudge and Pete are new in this neighborhood setting *is* important and this unfamiliarity affects how the characters achieve their goal. For example, a hilarious conversation develops with their new neighbor, Mrs. A, because she assumes that Uncle Feather is an uncle, rather than a pet.

✱ **When students can identify the components of a story, select the tiered activity that best fits each student in your classroom.**

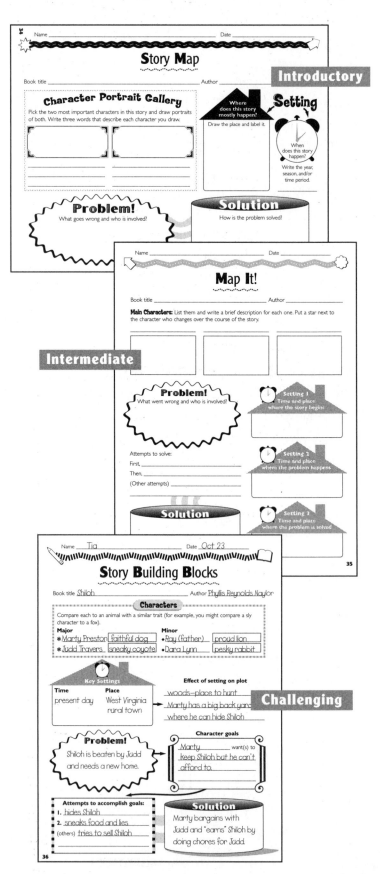

USING TIERED ACTIVITIES

Readers will:

* Select key story elements to fill in the organizer. [All]

* Sequence the events ("attempts") leading to the solution of the problem. [Intermediate and Challenging]

* Explain how the setting may have influenced the plot. [Challenging]

* Identify character goals and use these goals to see events as attempts to resolve a problem. [Challenging]

Graphic Organizers:

Introductory Level: Story Map (page 34)

Tip: Students may add additional characters to their Character Portrait Gallery by writing on the back of the page.

Intermediate Level: Map It! (page 35)

Challenging Level: Story Building Blocks (page 36)

Tip: Familiarize students with the terms *plot* (sequence of story events), *goals*, and *major* and *minor characters*.

Books Worth Using:

The Well by Mildred D. Taylor (Dial Books, 1995)

The Midwife's Apprentice by Karen Cushman (Clarion, 1995)

Mailing May by Michael O. Tunnell (Greenwillow Books, 1997) *Picture book*

Name _____ Date _____

Story Map

Book title _____

Author _____

Character Portrait Gallery

Pick the two most important characters in this story and draw portraits of both. Write three words that describe each character you draw.

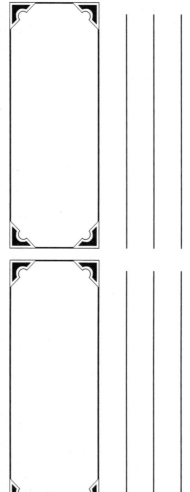

_____
_____
_____

_____
_____
_____

Setting

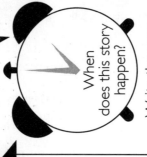

When does this story happen?

Write the year, season, and/or time period.

Where does this story mostly happen?

Draw the place and label it.

Solution

How is the problem solved?

Problem!

What goes wrong and who is involved?

Name _____ Date _____

Map It!

Book title _____ Author _____

Main Characters: List them and write a brief description for each one. Put a star next to the character who changes over the course of the story.

_____ _____ _____

[ ] [ ] [ ]

Problem!
What went wrong and who is involved?

Attempts to solve:

First, _____

Then, _____

(Other attempts) _____

_____

Solution

Setting 1
Time and place
where the story begins

Setting 2
Time and place
where the problem happens

Setting 3
Time and place
where the problem is solved

Story Building Blocks

Book title _____ Author _____

Characters

Compare each to an animal with a similar trait (for example, you might compare a sly character to a fox).

Major   **Minor**

✽ _____ [   ]   ◆ _____ [   ]

✽ _____ [   ]   ◆ _____ [   ]

Key Settings

Time   **Place**

Effect of setting on plot

_____

_____

_____

Problem!

Character goals

_____ want(s) to

_____

_____

_____

Attempts to accomplish goals:

1. _____

2. _____

(others) _____

_____

Solution

Character Analysis

Skill: *Show how character traits and actions affect or are affected by story events.*

About Character Analysis

When readers analyze a character, they identify and give meaning to that character's traits and actions. Good readers understand a character more fully by considering how the character is described; what the character says, does, and thinks; and how other characters react to him or her.

Why Is This Skill Important?

Character analysis allows the reader to look at what motivates the character to act as he or she does. Determining a character's motivations supports students' understanding of that character's role in the story and their ability to predict that character's behaviors in new situations. Further, character analysis gives students insights into the behaviors of important people in their own lives.

GETTING STARTED

Model Lesson: Analyzing characters with *Joey Pigza Swallowed the Key* by Jack Gantos (Farrar, Straus, & Giroux, 1998)

✳ **Introduce character analysis by explaining that in order to understand the way characters act, we look for special traits that tell us about their personalities.** Using a familiar character such as Charlotte from *Charlotte's Web* by E.B. White, I ask students to identify traits: "In three words, can you describe what kind of character Charlotte is?" We pick several of the traits we've listed and vote on scenes from the book that show how Charlotte's actions depict her traits.

✳ **Use a short passage rich in details that make a character's traits visible through his or her actions.** Using *Joey Pigza Swallowed the Key*—a story about a young boy with ADHD who truly wants to be good but keeps getting into trouble—I read a passage from Chapter 2 where the author uses actions and thoughts to describe Joey's traits:

> My morning pill was supposed to last all day but it gave out on me. I gripped the bottom of my chair and held tight and watched the second hand on the clock sweep around and around. And it wasn't that the important stuff Mrs. Maxy had to say went in one ear and out the other. It was that it didn't go in at all but just bounced off. And when the bell rang, I loosened my grip and blasted off for the door. (page 19)

After reading this passage, the class and I discuss what we know about

Joey: (1) he takes medication; (2) he is easily distracted; (3) he values learning; (4) he understands that he has a problem; and (5) he has lots of energy. We then identify information from the story that supports each character trait. For instance, we know that Joey values learning because he said that Mrs. Maxy was teaching "important stuff."

✳ **When students can name a character's traits and support their choices with actions from the story, match them with the appropriate tiered activities.** Students who are more advanced in this area will be able to anticipate a character's actions in a new situation, compare characters according to their traits, and differentiate between *dynamic* and *static* characters.

USING TIERED ACTIVITIES

Readers will:

❋ Name three character traits that fit a selected character. [All]

❋ Support each trait with details from the text, including character actions, thoughts, and words. [All]

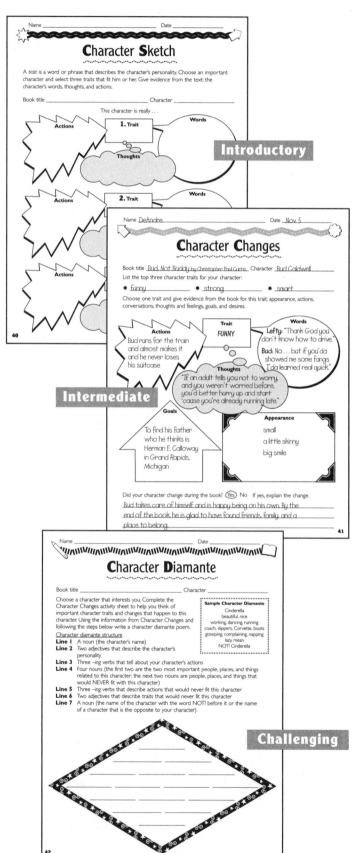

* Identify a change in the character and explain how the change affects the story. [Intermediate and Challenging]

* Compose a character diamante that supplies a characterization contrast with traits, actions, and associations "opposite" to the selected character. [Challenging]

Graphic Organizers:

Introductory Level: Character Sketch (page 40)

Intermediate Level: Character Changes (page 41)

Challenging Level: Character Diamante (page 42)

Tip: You may want students to first complete the Character Changes sheet so they have traits and evidence to use for their diamante poem. Students may need to review parts of speech before they can complete the poem.

Books Worth Using:

James and the Giant Peach by Roald Dahl (Puffin Books, 1961)

Island of the Blue Dolphins by Scott O'Dell (Dell, 1960)

Crazy Horse's Vision by Joseph Bruchac (Lee & Low Books, 2000) *Picture book*

Character Sketch

A *trait* is a word or phrase that describes the character's personality. Choose an important character and select three traits that fit him or her. Give evidence from the text: the character's words, thoughts, and actions.

Book title _____ Character _____

This character is really . . .

Actions

1. Trait

Thoughts

Words

Actions

2. Trait

Thoughts

Words

Actions

3. Trait

Thoughts

Words

Name _____ Date _____

Character Changes

Book title _____ Character _____

List the top three character traits for your character:

✹ _____ ✹ _____ ✹ _____

Choose one trait and give evidence from the book for this trait: appearance, actions, conversations, thoughts and feelings, goals, and desires.

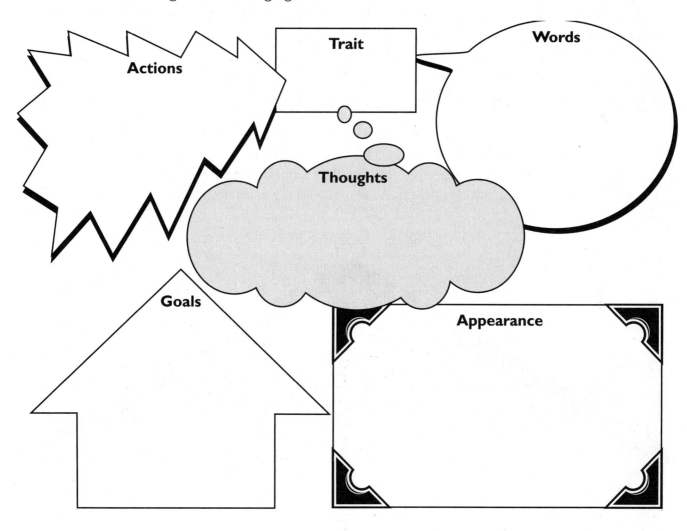

Actions

Trait

Words

Thoughts

Goals

Appearance

Did your character change during the book?   Yes   No   If yes, explain the change.

_____

_____

_____

Character Diamante

Book title _____ Character _____

Choose a character that interests you. Complete the Character Changes activity sheet to help you think of important character traits and changes that happen to this character. Using the information from Character Changes and following the steps below, write a character diamante poem.

Character diamante structure

Line 1 A noun (the character's name)

Line 2 Two adjectives that describe the character's personality

Line 3 Three *–ing* verbs that tell about your character's actions

Line 4 Four nouns (the first two are the two most important people, places, and things related to this character; the next two nouns are people, places, and things that would NEVER fit with this character)

Line 5 Three *–ing* verbs that describe actions that would never fit this character

Line 6 Two adjectives that describe traits that would never fit this character

Line 7 A noun (the name of the character with the word NOT! before it or the name of a character that is the opposite to your character)

> **Sample Character Diamante**
> Cinderella
> beautiful, nice
> working, dancing, running
> coach, slippers, Corvette, boots
> gossiping, complaining, napping
> lazy, mean
> NOT! Cinderella

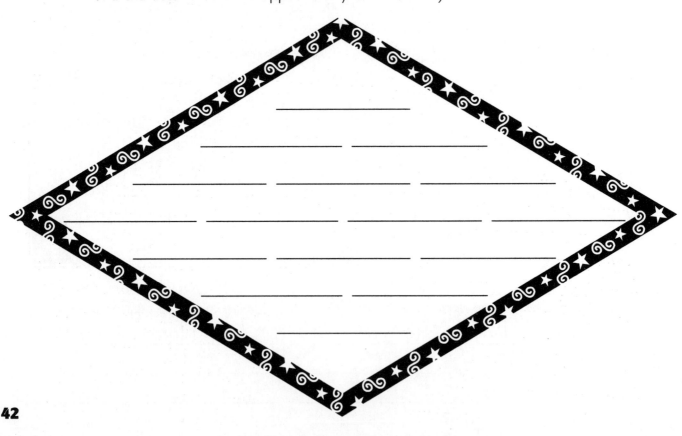

Character Perspective

Skill: *Show the perspectives of characters through support in the text (conversations, thoughts, and actions in response to events).*

About Character Perspective

When students identify a character's perspective, they show the character's views about particular events using the support of the character's actions, thoughts, and conversations. This skill builds on students' abilities to analyze characters: Students must use the information they know about the character (such as his or her traits) to examine the character's viewpoint about story events (see Character Analysis, page 37).

Why Is This Skill Important?

A character's perspective underlies his or her motives and actions in a text. Being able to identify actions that are "in character" will improve the accuracy of students' predictions.

GETTING STARTED

Model Lesson: Identifying character perspectives with *The War with Grandpa* by Robert Kimmel Smith (Dell Yearling, 1984)

* **Select an important event in a familiar text to introduce character perspective.** My students love the characters in *The War with Grandpa*, a story in which Grandpa comes to live with Pete's family and is given Pete's room. Pete is angry because he must sleep in the spooky attic room.

* **Lead students to identify key character actions, thoughts, and conversations that show how the character "sees" this event.** In *The War with Grandpa*, Pete starts the "war" by setting Grandpa's alarm at an early hour, making booby traps, and doing other things to get Grandpa to leave his space. Students easily identify Pete's actions and his resentful attitude toward the situation.

* **Help students clarify one character's perspective by contrasting it with another character's actions, thoughts, and conversations about the same event.** Using what we have learned in the text, I ask the students to compare Grandpa's reaction to taking Pete's room with Pete's reactions. (Students discover that Grandpa, too, dislikes the situation, but Pete does not realize this.)

Throughout the book Pete initiates incidents that sometimes amuse and other times anger Grandpa. At one point Pete steals Grandpa's slippers

and he writes a note saying, "You have been defeated" [*sic*]. I lead with these questions: "Are Pete's actions fair and is Grandpa's anger justified? What do you think about Grandpa's feelings in contrast to Pete's feelings?" Through this discussion students realize that Pete doesn't understand Grandpa's feelings and Grandpa doesn't understand how serious this intrusion is to Pete. When students advocate for Grandpa or Pete, it is evident they have ownership of character perspective.

✱ **Review perspective with a familiar fairy tale situation, where students can take on the perspective of one character or another.** I use "Goldilocks and the Three Bears" to see if students can reason how different characters might react over a given situation, such as the three bears' reactions to their porridge being eaten.

✱ **When students can offer answers that show they understand character perspectives, assign the appropriate tiered activities.**

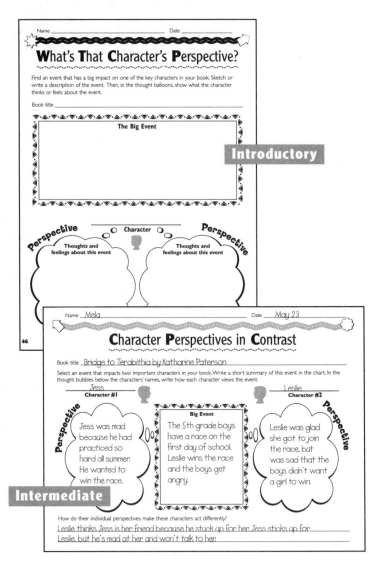

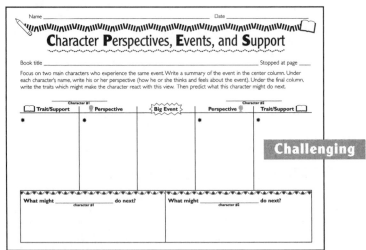

USING TIERED ACTIVITIES

Readers will:

❋ Summarize a key event. [All]

❋ Show how a character perceives a particular event. [All]

❋ Show how two characters perceive the same event differently and explain this difference in terms of unique perspectives. [Intermediate and Challenging]

❋ Identify and compare character traits that support the character's perspective. [Challenging]

Graphic Organizers:

Introductory Level: What's That Character's Perspective? (page 46)

Tip: Explain that cartoonists use thought balloons (the cloudlike bubbles above a character's head) to show what the character is thinking. Students should provide words related to what an important character in their story is thinking or feeling about an event. You might help students select a main character and a related key event that will provide them with enough material to determine that character's thoughts and feelings.

Intermediate Level: Character Perspectives in Contrast (page 47)

Tip: To emphasize different perspectives, encourage students to choose characters who have very different responses to the same event.

Challenging Level: Character Perspectives, Events, and Support (page 48)

Tip: Since this organizer requires students to predict a character's next action, make sure students note the point in their book at which they have stopped reading.

Books Worth Using:

Shiloh by Phyllis Reynolds Naylor (Atheneum, 1991)

A Solitary Blue by Cynthia Voigt (Scholastic, 1983)

Cinder Edna by Ellen Jackson (William Morrow & Co., 1994) *Picture book*

Name _____ Date _____

What's That Character's Perspective?

Find an event that has a big impact on one of the key characters in your book. Sketch or write a description of the event. Then, in the thought balloons, show what the character thinks or feels about the event.

Book title _____

The Big Event

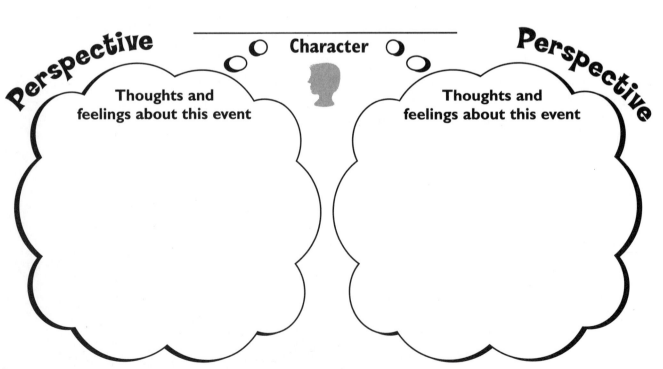

Perspective

Character _____

Perspective

Thoughts and feelings about this event

Thoughts and feelings about this event

Name _____

Date _____

Character Perspectives in Contrast

Book title _____

Select an event that impacts two important characters in your book. Write a short summary of this event in the chart. In the thought bubbles below the characters' names, write how each character views the event.

Character #2

Perspective

Big Event

Character #1

Perspective

How do their individual perspectives make these characters act differently? _____

Name _____

Date _____

Character Perspectives, Events, and Support

Book title _____

Stopped at page _____

Focus on two main characters who experience the same event. Write a summary of the event in the center column. Under each character's name, write his or her perspective (how he or she thinks and feels about the event). Under the final column, write the traits which might make the character react with this view. Then predict what this character might do next.

Character #1

Perspective

Trait/Support

✳

✳

Big Event

Character #2

Perspective

Trait/Support

✳

✳

What might _____ do next?

character #1

What might _____ do next?

character #2

Setting

Skill: *Analyze time and place details and explain the setting's influence on the story's plot.*

About Setting

Setting describes the time and location in which a story takes place. The author's choice of setting details influences the thoughts and actions of the characters and the line of the plot. This lesson moves students beyond simple identification of time and place details and helps them show how the setting influences the larger structure of the story.

Why Is This Skill Important?

Students need to understand that the setting influences characters' actions, dialogue and responses. More accomplished readers will understand that the setting may be affected by factors such as weather conditions and the attitudes of people who lived in the era in which the story takes place (e.g., attitudes toward land usage).

GETTING STARTED

Model Lesson: Analyzing setting with *Sing Down the Moon* by Scott O'Dell (Yearling Books, 1973)

By fourth grade, students can usually identify time and place details. I use plenty of examples of stories and passages rich with setting details and challenge them to think about how each setting uniquely shapes each story and its characters.

⁕ **Select a passage with detailed time and place elements that influence the action.** *Sing Down the Moon*, a historical fiction novel, focuses on a young Navaho girl's life from 1863 to 1865. This time in Navaho history includes "The Long Walk," when the United States government forced Navahos to leave their homeland, Arizona's Canyon de Chelly, and walk 300 miles to Fort Sumner, New Mexico. In *Sing Down the Moon*, the setting is integral to the plot of the book. The author develops the setting by contrasting the beauty of Canyon de Chelly with Fort Sumner. Changes in the setting are reflected in changes of attitudes among the Navaho characters.

⁕ **Identify components of the setting and show how these influence the story.** As I read the story with students, I think aloud to model how I'm keying into setting details that are important to the plot. I contrast the two settings and start to talk about the Navaho people's relationship with and experiences in each location. For example, Navaho traditions, such as respect for elders, were strong at the beginning of the book, when they lived in Canyon de Chelly, but, I point out, "When the Navaho are taken to Fort Sumner they act differently. They seem to lose their

spirit and give up. They are no longer the same people in this new setting." Through my comments and our discussion, the students understand that setting does influence the characters' feelings and actions.

✳ **Make sure students can apply what they know about setting.** I ask students, "Do you think this story could take place somewhere else or during another time?" I like using this question because it really gets them thinking about what happens in the plot and whether these actions could indeed take place in another era or another country.

✳ **When students can identify setting details and describe their effect on the story's plot, match them with the appropriate tiered activity.**

USING TIERED ACTIVITIES

Readers will:

❋ Identify the place and time of the story. [All]

❋ Explain why that setting is important to the story. [All]

❋ Explain how the setting affects a character's actions. [Intermediate and Challenging]

❋ Identify factors such as weather conditions and the attitudes of

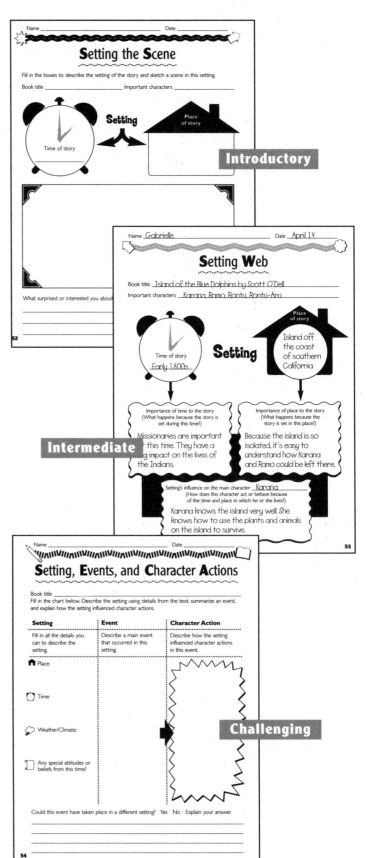

people who lived in the era in which the story takes place. [Challenging]

⁂ Summarize events that occurred and explain how the setting influenced the characters' actions. [Challenging]

Graphic Organizers:

Introductory Level: Setting the Scene (page 52)

Tip: Remind students that there may be multiple time and place details in the passage they're reading. For introductory and intermediate levels, encourage students to select and analyze only one setting from the story.

Intermediate Level: Setting Web (page 53)

Challenging Level: Setting, Events, and Character Actions (page 54)

Tip: Encourage students to consider two or three different settings from the story or passage. When they've completed the organizer, have them compare and contrast and discuss why the author may have selected these two or three settings.

••••••••••••••••••••••••••••••••••••••

Books Worth Using:

The Sign of the Beaver by Elizabeth George Speare (Yearling, 1983)

The Cage by Ruth Minsky Sender (Aladdin Paperbacks, 1986)

Painted Words, Spoken Memories by Aliki, (William Morrow & Co., 1994)
Picture book

Name _____ Date _____

Setting the Scene

Fill in the boxes to describe the setting of the story and sketch a scene in this setting.

Book title _____ Important characters _____

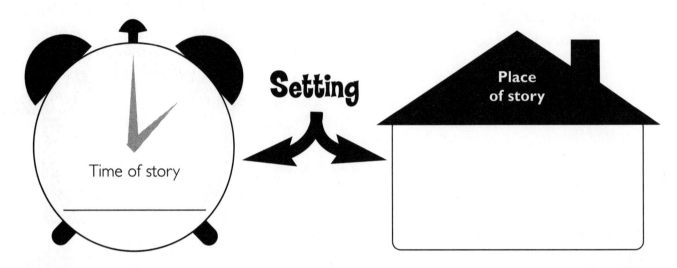

Time of story

_____

Setting

Place of story

Setting sketch

What surprised or interested you about this setting? If you could visit, would you want to?

_____

_____

_____

Name _____ Date _____

Setting Web

Book title _____

Important characters _____

Time of story

_____

Setting

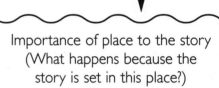

Place of story

↓ Importance of time to the story
(What happens because the story is
set during this time?)

↓ Importance of place to the story
(What happens because the
story is set in this place?)

Setting's influence on the main character, _____
(How does this character act or behave because
of the time and place in which he or she lives?)

Setting, Events, and Character Actions

Book title _____

Fill in the chart below. Describe the setting using details from the text, summarize an event, and explain how the setting influenced character actions.

Setting	Event	Character Action
Fill in all the details you can to describe the setting.	Describe a main event that occurred in this setting.	Describe how the setting influenced character actions in this event.

🏠 Place:

⏰ Time:

☁ Weather/Climate:

📜 Any special attitudes or beliefs from this time?

Could this event have taken place in a different setting?   Yes   No   Explain your answer.

_____

_____

_____

_____

Context Clues

Skill: *Determine the meaning of unfamiliar words using clues the author provides in the surrounding text.*

About Context Clues

Very seldom do we read lists of isolated words. More often than not, the words we read are placed in a context (i.e., they are surrounded by other words). Many times, the context provides enough information for us to determine the meaning of unfamiliar words. Authors use a variety of techniques, including comparing and contrasting ideas, providing examples, and embedding definitions in the text, to enable readers to understand unfamiliar words.

Why Is This Skill Important?

When they use context clues effectively, students can unlock the meaning of unfamiliar words, which helps them build vocabulary and more completely understand the text. We can help students become aware of how the context can support comprehension by providing examples of different types of context clues.

GETTING STARTED

Model Lesson: Using context clues with *Call It Courage* by Armstrong Sperry (Simon & Schuster, 1968)

* **Select and read aloud a passage with one or two unfamiliar words**

surrounded by helpful contextual clues. *Call It Courage* is the story of a young boy, Mafatu, whose fear of the sea causes other members of his island community to scorn him.

Throughout this book, Sperry provides rich context for vocabulary development. One example can be found in the following passage, when we begin to realize that Mafatu will never be able to overcome his fear of the sea nor contribute to the tribe as a fisherman. In this example, the reader can determine the meaning of two words: *coir* and *pursuits*.

> So, finally, he was not allowed to fare forth with the fishermen. He brought ill luck. He had to stay at home making spears and nets, twisting coir—the husk of the coconut—into stout sharkline for other boys to use. He became very skillful at these pursuits, but he hated them. (pages 7–8)

* **Point out signs that often indicate context clues are present.** I explain that punctuation is sometimes used to help readers figure out the meaning of unfamiliar words. For example, when I see an em dash (—) following a word I don't know, I simply continue to read, realizing that the word will probably be defined and followed by another em dash, as is the case with

the word *coir* above. I provide students with additional examples and ask them to be on the lookout for other instances in which punctuation (em dashes, parentheses, or commas) is used for this purpose.

I continue by explaining that in order for me to determine the meaning of *pursuits* I need to weave together several pieces of information. I model my thinking process: "The author lets me know that rather than being with the fishermen, Mafatu is 'making spears and nets, twisting coir.'" I continue, "I also know that he was 'very skillful at these pursuits.'" I explain that these two pieces of information lead me to believe that *pursuits* has something to do with Mafatu's work.

Although students can determine the meanings of these two target words from the context, I caution that the context will not always help them unlock the meaning of unfamiliar words. In the following example from this book, for instance, the word *luminous* cannot be defined from the context: "Now the air was luminous with promise of another day. Out of the sultry mists . . ." (page 26). We search for other examples of contexts that are useful and not useful in defining unfamiliar words.

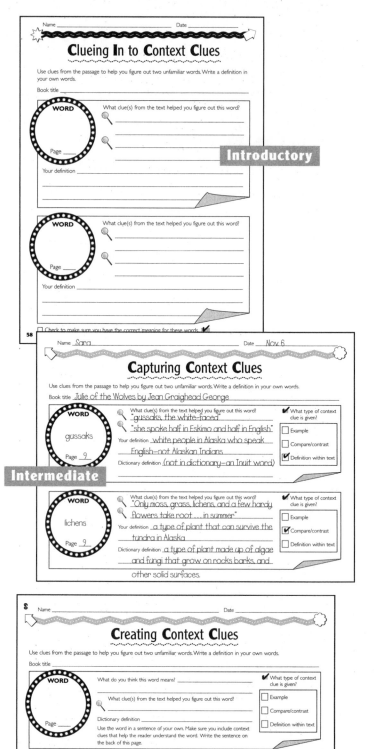

* Once students have been exposed to various types of context clues, and can demonstrate through guided practice that they understand how to use them, match them with the appropriate tiered activities.

USING TIERED ACTIVITIES

Readers will:

* Analyze the context to unlock the meaning of two unfamiliar words. [All]

* List the clues that the author provided to help determine each word's meaning. [All]

* Define the target words. [All]

* Verify their definitions with another person (friend, teacher, aide, or parent). [Introductory]

* Verify their definitions with a dictionary. [Intermediate and Challenging]

* Identify the type of context clue used by the author. [Intermediate and Challenging]

* Apply knowledge of the new words by creating original sentences, incorporating context clues that can help illustrate the words' meanings. [Challenging]

Graphic Organizers:

Introductory Level: Clueing In to Context Clues (page 58)

Tip: Let students know how they should check their definitions (e.g., confirm with a friend, teacher, aide, parent, and/or dictionary).

Intermediate Level: Capturing Context Clues (page 59)

Tip: Make sure that students understand the definitions of the different types of context clues. "Within text" is used for *embedded definition*.

Challenging Level: Creating Context Clues (page 60)

Tip: To check their work, have students read their sentences to a partner to see if the partner can define the word from its context.

Books Worth Using:

Don't You Know There's a War On? by Avi (HarperCollins, 2001)

No Promises in the Wind by Irene Hunt (Berkley, 1970)

Uncle Jed's Barbershop by Margaree King Mitchell (Simon & Schuster, 1993)
Picture book

Name _____ Date _____

Clueing In to Context Clues

Use clues from the passage to help you figure out two unfamiliar words. Write a definition in your own words.

Book title _____

WORD

Page _____

What clue(s) from the text helped you figure out this word?

_____

_____

_____

Your definition _____

_____

_____

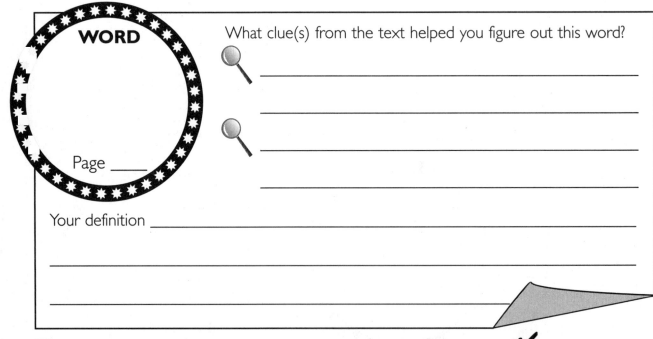

WORD

Page _____

What clue(s) from the text helped you figure out this word?

_____

_____

_____

Your definition _____

_____

_____

☐ Check to make sure you have the correct meaning for these words. ✔

Date _____

Capturing Context Clues

Use clues from the passage to help you figure out two unfamiliar words. Write a definition in your own words.

Book title _____

WORD

Page _____

🔍 🔍 What clue(s) from the text helped you figure out this word? _____

Your definition _____

Dictionary definition _____

✓ What type of context clue is given?

☐ Example

☐ Compare/contrast

☐ Definition within text

WORD

Page _____

🔍 🔍 What clue(s) from the text helped you figure out this word? _____

Your definition _____

Dictionary definition _____

✓ What type of context clue is given?

☐ Example

☐ Compare/contrast

☐ Definition within text

Creating Context Clues

Use clues from the passage to help you figure out two unfamiliar words. Write a definition in your own words.

Book title _____

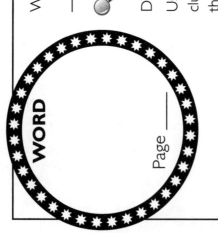

WORD

Page _____

What type of context clue is given?

☐ Example

☐ Compare/contrast

☐ Definition within text

What do you think this word means? _____

What clue(s) from the text helped you figure out this word? _____

Dictionary definition _____

Use the word in a sentence of your own. Make sure you include context clues that help the reader understand the word. Write the sentence on the back of this page.

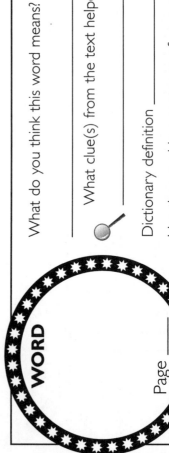

WORD

Page _____

What type of context clue is given?

☐ Example

☐ Compare/contrast

☐ Definition within text

What do you think this word means? _____

What clue(s) from the text helped you figure out this word? _____

Dictionary definition _____

Use the word in a sentence of your own. Make sure you include context clues that help the reader understand the word. Write the sentence on the back of this page.

Problem and **S**olution

Skill: *Identify problems and solutions within a text and explain whether the solutions aided the characters in reaching their goals.*

About Problem and Solution

The problem and the solution of a story are the simplest forms of the plot: the rising action leading to the climax of the story, followed by the resolution. A character's attempts to solve the problem and reach his or her goal are the basis for excitement and suspense within texts.

Why Is This Skill Important?

Understanding the plot of a story is the most important factor in comprehending the text. To understand the story, students need to comprehend what is happening in the story, why it is happening, and what actions and reactions the events are causing.

GETTING STARTED

Model Lesson: Identifying problems and solutions with *Journey of the Sparrows* by Fran Leeper Buss (Dell Publishing, 1991)

* **Choose a book with a story line that makes identifying the problems and solutions easy.** I use *Journey of the Sparrows*, a book about a teenage girl who, along with an older sister and younger brother, illegally crosses the Mexican border only to find a meager existence working at a sweatshop factory in Chicago. Problems surround their journey to Chicago, their life in Chicago, and their attempts to bring their mother and baby sister across the border.

* **Point out that goals often drive the plot, causing characters to act in ways that create problems or that counteract existing problems.** We discuss Maria's goal: to bring her entire family to Chicago. Explain that acting on this goal is dangerous both physically and legally and threatens to break the family apart for good.

* **Help students identify problems and generate probable solutions.** As I read this book with the class we list each problem, generate possible solutions, and then read on to see if the author used one of our solutions. (The structure and topic of *Journey of the Sparrows* support the frequent use of this prediction strategy; throughout the story the immigrants encounter numerous problems for which they must find solutions.) When students read about Maria attempting to cross the border with her baby sister, they are able to identify several solutions: She can

wade and swim across the Rio Grande with the baby, she can pay for a ride with a "coyote" (a driver willing to sneak them across the border), or she can pay for someone to row them across. The solution that would enable Maria to obtain her goal—that of getting herself and the baby safely back to Chicago—is not clear. This makes for both a great reading and a real-world lesson: Students must assess, along with Maria, which might be the safest choice.

✷ **When students are able to identify a character's goal and the related problems that character faces, and evaluate the solutions, select a tiered activity that best meets each learner's needs.**

USING TIERED ACTIVITIES

Readers will:

❉ Identify the main problem and the solution. [All]

❉ Explain whether the solution aided the character in obtaining that goal. [All]

❉ Write alternative solutions that could solve the problem. [Intermediate and Challenging]

❉ Compare the story solution with alternative solutions. [Intermediate and Challenging]

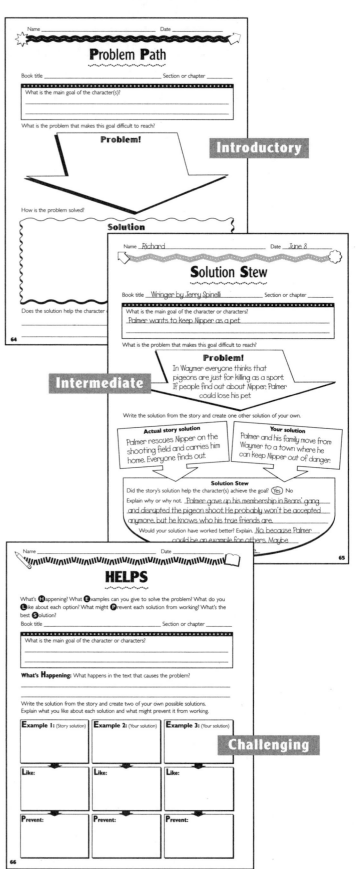

* Evaluate the advantages and disadvantages of possible solutions. [Challenging]

* Decide which solution is best and explain how this would help the character or characters achieve the goal. [Challenging]

Graphic Organizers:

Introductory Level: Problem Path (page 64)

Intermediate Level: Solution Stew (page 65)

Challenging Level: HELPS (page 66)

Tip: In the Example category, students should provide probable and valid ideas they have thought of to help the character or characters.

Books Worth Using:

Far North by Will Hobbs (Avon Camelot, 1996)

Sweet Clara and the Freedom Quilt by Deborah Hopkinson, (Dragon Fly Books, 1993) *Picture book*

The War with Grandpa by Robert Kimmel Smith (Dell Yearling, 1984)

Problem **P**ath

Book title _____ Section or chapter _____

★★★

What is the main goal of the character(s)?

_____

_____

What is the problem that makes this goal difficult to reach?

Problem!

How is the problem solved?

Solution

Does the solution help the character or characters achieve the main goal? Explain.

_____

_____

Solution Stew

Book title _____ Section or chapter _____

★★

What is the main goal of the character or characters?

_____

_____

What is the problem that makes this goal difficult to reach?

Problem!

Write the solution from the story and create one other solution of your own.

Actual story solution

Your solution

Solution Stew

Did the story's solution help the character(s) achieve the goal?   Yes   No

Explain why or why not. _____

_____

_____

Would your solution have worked better? Explain. _____

_____

HELPS

What's **H**appening? What **E**xamples can you give to solve the problem? What do you **L**ike about each option? What might **P**revent each solution from working? What's the best **S**olution?

Book title _____ Section or chapter _____

★★★

What is the main goal of the character or characters?

_____

_____

What's Happening: What happens in the text that causes the problem?

_____

_____

Write the solution from the story and create two of your own possible solutions.
Explain what you like about each solution and what might prevent it from working.

Example 1: (Story solution)	**Example 2:** (Your solution)	**Example 3:** (Your solution)
Like:	**Like:**	**Like:**
Prevent:	**Prevent:**	**Prevent:**

Details

Skill: *Examine texts for detail-rich passages.*

About Details

According to the Merriam-Webster Dictionary (1997), details are the "extended treatment of or attention to particular items." Authors give this extended treatment to important parts of their writing to develop and clarify ideas. Details are often included in a piece of fiction to move the story line along, or to reveal something about a character, setting, problem, conflict, or resolution.

Why Is This Skill Important?

Concentrating on a text's details helps students better visualize the content and focuses attention on explicit or implicit information. Furthermore, students who have experience reading richly detailed pieces may transfer their understanding of the author's craft to their own writing.

GETTING STARTED

Model Lesson: Examining details with *Pink and Say* by Patricia Polacco (Philomel Books, 1994)

* **Read aloud from an engaging, short passage.** In *Pink and Say*, Patricia Polacco reconstructs a relationship that forms between two boys—one black and one white—during the Civil War. She provides

readers with rich details of their journey together, as friends and young soldiers. Take, for example, the following passage. It takes place just after Pinkus (Pink) has found Sheldon (Say) so badly wounded that he can't walk on his own:

> I remember being pulled and carried, and stumblin'. I remember hard branches snappin' back in my face and mouths full of dirt as we hit the ground to keep from being seen. I remember sloggin' through streams, haulin' up small bluffs and belly-crawlin' through dry fields. I remember these things in half-sleeplike, but I do remember being carried for a powerful long way. (unpaged)

* **Emphasize the power in using detail to enrich a text.** I point out that Polacco could simply have written, "Say was carried by Pink a long way through all kinds of weather and terrain"—and leave it at that. But by adding specific details, she lets us "see" in our mind's eye exactly what it was like for Say to be carried by Pink. I explain that details help us realize how long and arduous the trip was. I tell students how I came to this conclusion: I explain that Say was only partially conscious. I ask them to share what it's like to carry a sleeping

child and to relate this to Say's condition and Pink's effort to carry him "a powerful long way."

I reread the part about the hard branches and the mouths full of dirt. I help students see that through carefully crafted details, the author revealed information about character traits (Pink's bravery and strength), setting (wilderness in dangerous, rebel-controlled territory), and other story elements.

* **Use a snapshot metaphor to illustrate how an author employs details to focus the reader's attention.** Next, I show two photographs: one that is bright and clear, and another that is out of focus. I explain that when we take a snapshot with a camera, we want to be able to home in on a particular thing, person, or place and see the physical details clearly.

* **Invite students to offer colorful descriptions of their own.** In writing, we can use the same idea of a "snapshot" (Lane, 1993) to help us see what is being described. To do this, we need clear, vivid details. We can add details, even to a rich passage, to make it more focused. For instance, suppose an author wrote, "I rollerbladed cautiously through a throng of poky

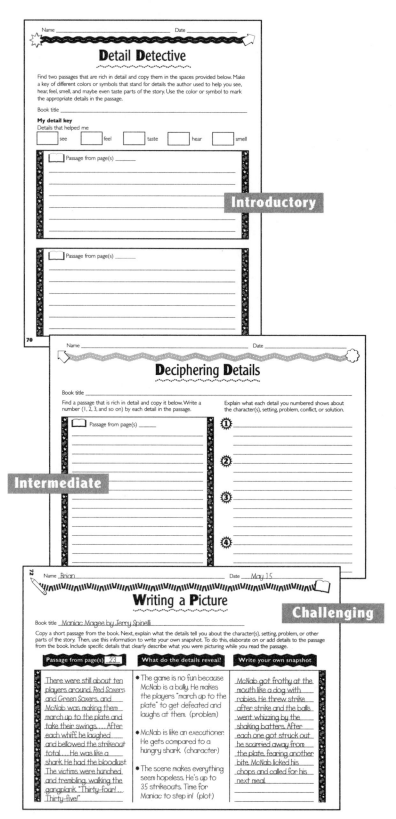

tourists who strolled along Perkins Avenue." The following snapshot reveals more of what I'm picturing about the setting: "I rollerbladed cautiously through a throng of poky tourists, who had expensive cameras hanging from their necks. They strolled along Perkins Avenue, peeking into the windows of the tastefully decorated gift shops that lined the quaint street." I invite students to revise and share examples from their own writing. This activity prepares students for the Writing a Picture organizer.

✳ **When students have demonstrated an understanding of how details are used to create a picture in the reader's mind and focus the reader's attention, match them with the appropriate tiered activities.**

USING TIERED ACTIVITIES

Readers will:

❀ Find and examine richly detailed passages. [All]

❀ Explain what the details reveal about the character, setting, conflict, problem, and resolution. Analyze how details allow the author to divulge explicit or implicit information. [Intermediate and Challenging]

❀ Use the snapshot technique to revise a passage from the book. [Challenging]

Graphic Organizers:

Introductory Level: Detail Detective (page 70)

Intermediate Level: Deciphering Details (page 71)

Tip: Be sure students understand the terminology used in the directions (e.g., *conflict, solution*).

Challenging Level: Writing a Picture (page 72)

. . . .

Books Worth Using:

In the Year of the Boar and Jackie Robinson by Bette Bao Lord (Harper Trophy, 1984)

A Wrinkle in Time by Madeleine L'Engle (Farrar Straus & Giroux, Inc., 1962)

When Jessie Came Across the Sea by Amy Hest (Scholastic, 1997) *Picture book*

Name _____   Date _____

Detail **D**etective

Find two passages that are rich in detail and copy them in the spaces provided below. Make a key of different colors or symbols that stand for details the author used to help you see, hear, feel, smell, and maybe even taste parts of the story. Use the color or symbol to mark the appropriate details in the passage.

Book title _____

My detail key

Details that helped me

| | see | | feel | | taste | | hear | | smell |

📖 Passage from page(s) _____

_____

_____

_____

_____

_____

_____

📖 Passage from page(s) _____

_____

_____

_____

_____

_____

_____

Name _____

Date _____

Deciphering Details

Book title _____

Find a passage that is rich in detail and copy it below. Write a number (1, 2, 3, and so on) by each detail in the passage.

📖 Passage from page(s) _____

Explain what each detail you numbered shows about the character(s), setting, problem, conflict, or solution.

① _____

② _____

③ _____

④ _____

Name _____

Date _____

Writing a Picture

Book title _____

Copy a short passage from the book. Next, explain what the details tell you about the character(s), setting, problem, or other parts of the story. Then, use this information to write your own snapshot. To do this, elaborate on or add details to the passage from the book. Include specific details that clearly describe what you were picturing while you read the passage.

Passage from page(s) [___]

What do the details reveal?

Write your own snapshot

Point of View

Skill: *Recognize the author's point of view and determine how this influences the story.*

About Point of View

Point of view is how an author decides to tell a story. There are two commonly used points of view. One is called the third-person, or *omniscient*, point of view, meaning "all knowing." In this case, the author gives the reader knowledge of what all the characters are thinking. The other point of view, which is called *first person*, tells the story in the words of one of the characters. When an author writes from a first-person viewpoint, she can provide alternative points of view by allowing different characters to speak.

Why Is This Skill Important?

Students need to understand that the author has deliberately chosen a certain point of view. Readers should know who is telling the story, and how using this point of view influences the story.

GETTING STARTED

Model Lesson: Recognizing point of view in *The Music of Dolphins* by Karen Hesse (Scholastic, 1996) and in *Lyddie* by Katherine Paterson (Puffin Books, 1991)

* **Introduce the third-person point of view.** I use two different books to teach point of view. I begin with the book *Lyddie*, a novel about young girls working mill jobs in Lowell, Massachusetts. Using the third person, Paterson gives us information on four characters as she writes: "Amelia corralled Lyddie and Prudence for long walks along the river before it grew too dark. Betsey, of course, did whatever she liked regardless of Amelia." (page 79) Discuss with the class what the author is telling us about each character. We learn that Amelia is friendly and energetic and likes to walk. Lyddie and Prudence are agreeable and friendly and will go with Amelia. Betsey, on the other hand, seems to be independent and does not walk with the girls. I point out that we can learn a little about each character the author chooses to focus on through an outside observer perspective. So, even though the book focuses on Lyddie's story, we hear *about* her; she does not tell us directly what is in her heart and mind.

* **Introduce the first-person point of view.** To compare this to a first-person narrative, I use the book *The Music of Dolphins* by Karen Hesse. The book is about Mila, a teenager, who was found on an isolated island where she had been raised by dolphins. Interestingly, the reader can follow

Mila's humanization by her growth in speech throughout the chapters. The poignancy of the story is dependent on Mila's perspective as she views life through the lens of the dolphin culture in which she was raised. To illustrate the effect of a first-person narrative, I use the following passage, where Mila is talking about her concept of family to Sandy, her caretaker.

> I have another family too. Dolphin family. The ones who love and care for me. The ones I love and care for. Can they see me again? I say, Sandy, can the dolphins see me again? (page 15)

We discuss Mila's feelings and ideas. She believes that since the dolphins loved and cared for her, they are family. Mila loves the dolphins, misses them, and wants to see them again. I ask, "Because this is written in first person, what don't we know?" In this case, the reader does not know what Sandy thinks about this. We also do not have an opportunity to see Mila through an outside-observer lens. We discuss that when a story is written in first person, we learn about the story through a one-character perspective.

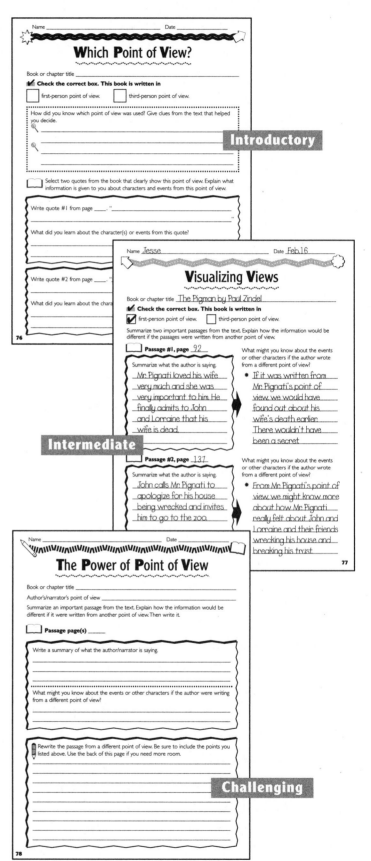

* **Work together to identify different points of view.** Before having students work independently on point of view, I have them work in pairs and discuss the following sentences. They must be able to explain whether the sentences are written in first or third person and how that influences the information the reader receives. The partners then discuss their ideas with the class.

> It seems that I am always calling my friends and they never call me. (first)
>
> Colleen, Kaitlin, and Tasha were talking next to the water fountain. Tasha didn't tell the others she had a date that night. (third)
>
> Andy and Tomas put on their coats and walked out the door arm-in-arm. Andy was glad his friend had forgiven him. Tomas knew he had done the right thing. (third)
>
> "Don't people understand why I do these things?" I thought. "Don't they know I just don't know what else to do?" (first)

* **When students can distinguish between first-person and third-person narration, match them with the appropriate tiered activity.**

USING TIERED ACTIVITIES

Readers will:

* Identify the author's point of view and explain how this informs the reader. [All]

* Explain how the author can slant information depending on the view by stating what may be missing or misleading. [Intermediate and Challenging]

* Synthesize information to rewrite a passage from a new point of view. [Challenging]

Graphic Organizers:

Introductory Level: Which Point of View? (page 76)

Intermediate Level: Visualizing Views (page 77)

Challenging Level: The Power of Point of View (page 78)

Tip: Make it clear that at the intermediate and challenging levels, students must use their imaginations to make inferences when writing from a different point of view.

Books Worth Using:

Moon Over Tennessee by Craig Crist-Evans (Houghton Mifflin, 1999)

The Pigman by Paul Zindel (Bantam Books, 1968)

Rocks in His Head by Carol Otis Hurst (Greenwillow Books, 2001) *Picture book*

Name _____ Date _____

Which Point of View?

Book or chapter title _____

✔ **Check the correct box. This book is written in**

☐ first-person point of view.   ☐ third-person point of view.

How did you know which point of view was used? Give clues from the text that helped you decide.

🔍 _____

🔍 _____

_____

_____

📖 Select two quotes from the book that clearly show this point of view. Explain what information is given to you about characters and events from this point of view.

Write quote #1 from page _____. "_____

_____ "

What did you learn about the character(s) or events from this quote?

_____

_____

Write quote #2 from page _____. "_____

_____ "

What did you learn about the character(s) or events from this quote?

_____

_____

Visualizing Views

Book or chapter title _____

✔ **Check the correct box. This book is written in**

☐ first-person point of view. ☐ third-person point of view.

Summarize two important passages from the text. Explain how the information would be different if the passages were written from another point of view.

Passage #1, page _____

Summarize what the author is saying.

_____

_____

_____

_____

_____

_____

_____

What might you know about the events or other characters if the author wrote from a different point of view?

✱ _____

_____

_____

_____

_____

_____

Passage #2, page _____

Summarize what the author is saying.

_____

_____

_____

_____

_____

What might you know about the events or other characters if the author wrote from a different point of view?

✱ _____

_____

_____

_____

_____

The Power of Point of View

Book or chapter title _____

Author's/narrator's point of view _____

Summarize an important passage from the text. Explain how the information would be different if it were written from another point of view. Then write it.

Passage page(s) _____

Write a summary of what the author/narrator is saying.

_____

_____

_____

What might you know about the events or other characters if the author were writing from a different point of view?

_____

_____

Rewrite the passage from a different point of view. Be sure to include the points you listed above. Use the back of this page if you need more room.

_____

_____

_____

_____

_____

_____

_____

_____

Cause and Effect

Skill: *Identify cause-and-effect relationships in narrative texts.*

About Cause and Effect

Cause and effect is a relationship that writers use to show "how facts, events, or concepts (effects) happen or come into being because of other facts, events, or concepts (causes)" (Vacca and Vacca, 1993, page 41). In other words, *cause* is any event or action that produces a result. The result is the *effect*. Sometimes causes and effects are clearly stated. In such instances, the author may use signal words including *because*, *since*, and *consequently*. At other times, however, the relationship may only be implied.

Why Is This Skill Important?

Students need to understand the relationship between events and their consequences in order to make logical story connections.

GETTING STARTED

Model Lesson: Introducing cause and effect with *The Giver* by Lois Lowry (Houghton Mifflin, 1993)

* **Introduce the concept of cause and effect with examples that relate to students' experiences.** I begin by introducing a few real-life examples of cause-and-effect

relationships: (1) Dave was not allowed to practice with the track team (effect) because he had the flu (cause). (2) Since Tatianna knew how to burn a CD (cause), all her friends expected her to make copies for them (effect).

Identifying cause-and-effect relationships can be difficult at first. You may need to model several examples of this strategy using words such as *action* (for cause) and *result* (for effect) before students are able to work independently.

* **Read aloud from an engaging short passage.** Once I feel that students are comfortable with the cause-and-effect concept, I introduce examples of implicit relationships. On page 46 of *The Giver*, readers find out that when children in this fictional community turn ten years old, they get their hair cut.

> . . . each child's hair was snipped neatly into its distinguishing cut: females lost their braids at Ten, and the males, too, relinquished their long childish hair and took on the more manly short style which exposed their ears.

* **Help students identify the cause and the effect.** I explain that the cause (action) is turning ten years

old. The effect (result) is a new hairstyle that signals the end of youth. This cause-and-effect relationship is a bit more abstract than the two examples at the beginning of the lesson, where signal words are used to indicate the relationship. Here, readers must infer the connection between ideas.

I tell my students that I sometimes like to imagine that the action (cause) produces a different result (effect) than the one the author uses in a story. In this case, turning ten (the action) could lead to many results. The ten-year-olds in this book could be given more free time and less regulated tasks; they might be excused from one of the community rituals. I ask, "What else could happen when these children turn ten?" and students brainstorm other possible effects. This activity helps students prepare for the Effective Effects and Going Beyond Cause and Effect organizers.

✳ **After students are able to identify causes and effects in the examples you provide, match them with the appropriate tiered activities.**

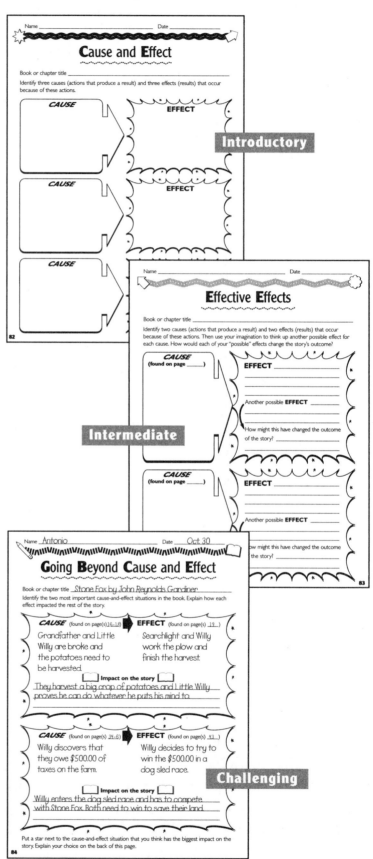

80

USING TIERED ACTIVITIES

Readers will:

❋ Identify causes and related effects in a story. [All]

❋ Assume a writer's perspective and create a plausible alternative effect for each of the three causes they've identified. [Intermediate]

❋ Explain how each alternative effect might have changed the outcome of the story. [Intermediate]

❋ Determine which of the actual effects from the story had the biggest impact on the story's outcome. [Challenging]

Graphic Organizers:

Introductory Level: Cause and Effect (page 82)

Tip: You can scaffold this assignment for students by selecting and filling in either the cause or the effect.

Intermediate Level: Effective Effects (page 83)

Challenging Level: Going Beyond Cause and Effect (page 84)

••••••••••••••••••••••••••••••••••

Books Worth Using:

Nowhere to Call Home by Cynthia DeFelice (Farrar, Straus & Giroux, 1999)

That Was Then, This Is Now by S. E. Hinton (Dell Publishing, 1971)

Keep the Lights Burning, Abbie by Peter and Connie Roop (Carolrhoda Books, 1985) *Picture book*

Name _____ Date _____

Cause and Effect

Book or chapter title _____

Identify three causes (actions that produce a result) and three effects (results) that occur because of these actions.

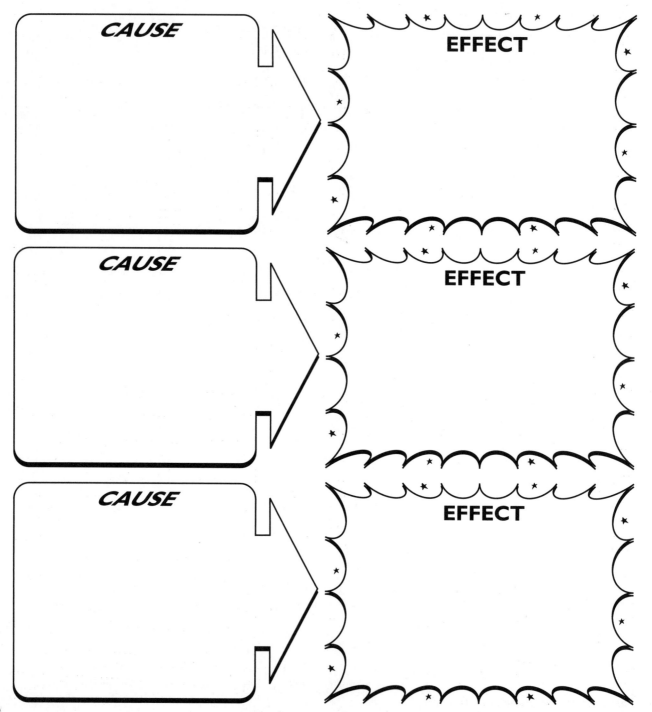

CAUSE

EFFECT

CAUSE

EFFECT

CAUSE

EFFECT

Name _____ Date _____

Effective Effects

Book or chapter title _____

Identify two causes (actions that produce a result) and two effects (results) that occur because of these actions. Then use your imagination to think up another possible effect for each cause. How would each of your "possible" effects change the story's outcome?

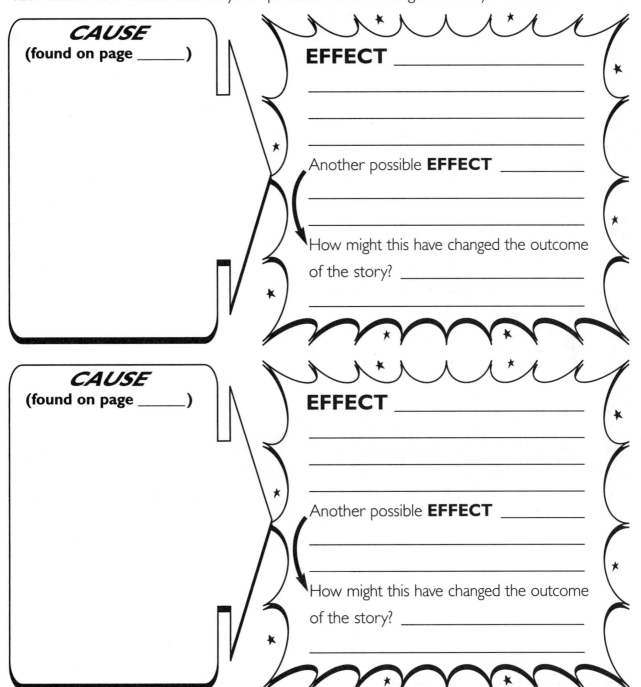

CAUSE
(found on page _____)

EFFECT _____
_____
_____
_____

Another possible **EFFECT** _____
_____
_____
How might this have changed the outcome of the story? _____
_____

CAUSE
(found on page _____)

EFFECT _____
_____
_____
_____

Another possible **EFFECT** _____
_____
_____
How might this have changed the outcome of the story? _____
_____

Going Beyond Cause and Effect

Book or chapter title _____

Identify the two most important cause-and-effect situations in the book. Explain how each effect impacted the rest of the story.

★ ★

CAUSE (found on page(s) ___) ➡ **EFFECT** (found on page(s) ___)

★

★

Impact on the story

★

★

_____

_____

_____

★ ★

★ ★

CAUSE (found on page(s) ___) ➡ **EFFECT** (found on page(s) ___)

★

★

Impact on the story

★

★

_____

_____

_____

★ ★

Put a star next to the cause-and-effect situation that you think has the biggest impact on the story. Explain your choice on the back of this page.

Compare and Contrast

Skill: *Identify the similarities and differences between two characters, settings, or other story elements in a text or texts.*

About Compare and Contrast

Comparing and contrasting elements in narrative texts involves identifying how story elements, situations, and plots are alike and different. Comparing likenesses and differences helps readers make connections and draw distinctions between key elements in a story.

Why Is This Skill Important?

Analyzing the differences and similarities in story components helps students focus on details that cause certain actions or results in the story. This gives them a greater understanding of the text.

GETTING STARTED

Model Lesson: Comparing and contrasting characters in *Holes* by Louis Sachar (Yearling Books, 1998)

* **Introduce the idea of comparing and contrasting with simple object models.** I use a Venn diagram (page 88) to compare two different objects like shoes or backpacks. In the outer circles we note the differences between the objects, and in the area where the circles intersect we note the similarities. My next step is to use a compare-and-contrast organizer to map out familiar story elements such

as character traits. For instance, when I want to compare and contrast two characters, I start by inviting students to analyze two well-developed characters from a passage or passages in which students do not struggle with the text. (See also Character Analysis lesson, page 37.)

* **Read aloud from an engaging short passage.** In the book *Holes*, an innocent but unlucky adolescent, Stanley, is sent to a juvenile detention "camp" as punishment for stealing. There, he and his fellow "campers" are made to dig a five-foot hole daily. Using this book, I model comparing and contrasting by focusing on the actions and dialogue of two minor (but strongly articulated) characters: the Warden and Mr. Sir, the camp guard. In the following passage, the Warden, knowing she is close to finding her treasure, demands harder work from the young boys:

> By lunchtime the Warden was beginning to lose her patience. She made them eat quickly, so they could get back to work. "If you can't get them to work any faster," she told Mr. Sir, "then you're going to have to climb down there and dig with them."
>
> After that, everyone worked faster, especially when Mr. Sir was watching

them. Stanley practically ran when he pushed his wheelbarrow. Mr. Sir reminded them that they weren't Girl Scouts. (page 73)

✳ **Help students compare and contrast on their own.** To help my students compare and contrast, we first identify the Warden's traits: impatient, bossy, and inconsiderate. We can see that Mr. Sir is subservient to the Warden, frightening to the boys, insensitive, and observant. To find similarities, I ask, "How are the Warden and Mr. Sir alike? I see that they both can boss the boys. What other things do you see as the same?" Students offer responses such as: They are both mean, neither cares about the boys, and both want to get the job done. I explain the importance of these similarities and differences to the plot, and how they help us to predict the behavior of the characters.

We can now easily move from the Venn Diagram to the Compare Chart organizer, where I show students how to record the evidence from the text that supports our comparisons.

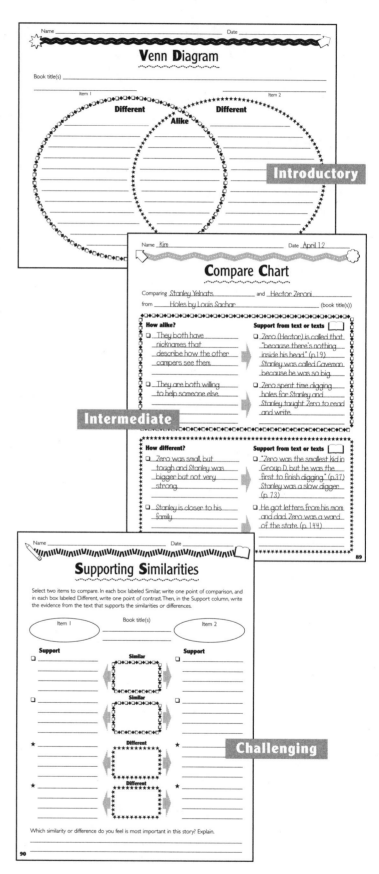

✳ **When students can use details from the text to compare and contrast two characters or any other two story elements, match them with the appropriate tiered activities.**

USING TIERED ACTIVITIES

Readers will:

❀ Label the two areas being compared, and list details that show how these areas are alike and different. [All]

❀ Support their ideas with evidence from the text or texts. [Intermediate and Challenging]

❀ Think critically and determine categorical elements common or different to both areas (such as honesty as a character trait, or friendship as a theme) in two texts. [Challenging]

❀ Evaluate which similarity or difference is the most significant, and explain why. [Challenging]

Graphic Organizers:

Introductory Level: Venn Diagram (page 88)

Intermediate Level: Compare Chart (page 89)

Challenging Level: Supporting Similarities (Adapted from Swartz and Parks, 1994) (page 90)

Tip: When using the Supporting Similarities activity, show the students a completed sample before they do their own.

Books Worth Using:

True North by Kathryn Lasky (The Blue Sky Press, 1996)

Among the Hidden by Margaret Peterson Haddix (Aladdin, 1998)

When Pigasso Met Mootise by Nina Laden (Chronicle Books, 1998) *Picture book*

Name _____

Date _____

Venn Diagram

Book title(s) _____

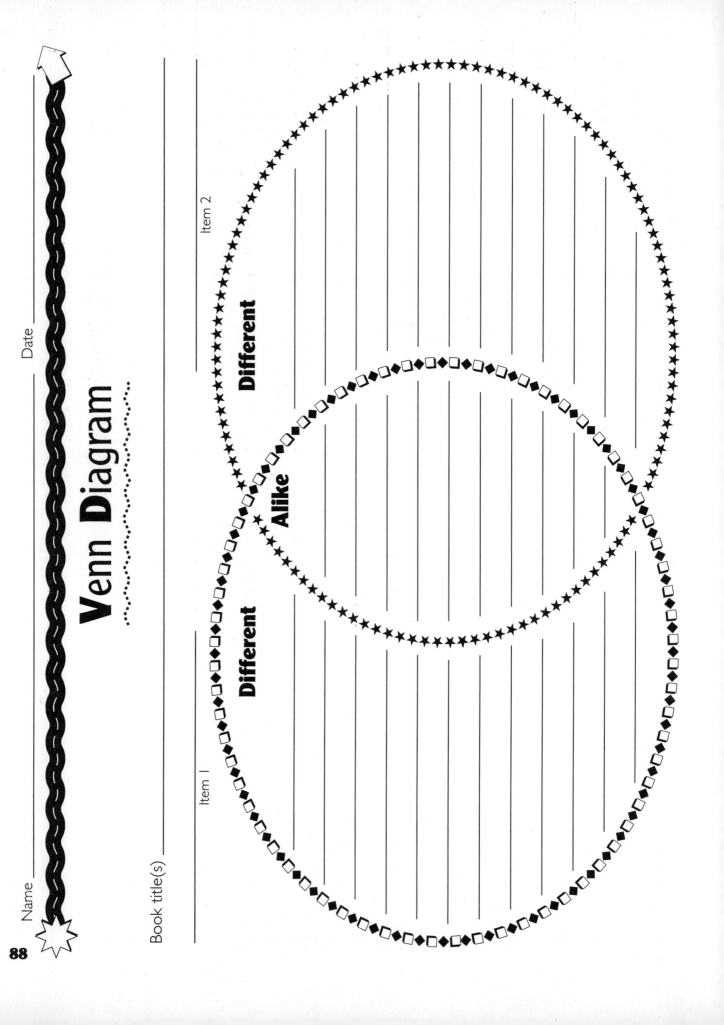

Item 1

Item 2

Different

Alike

Different

Name _____ Date _____

Compare Chart

Comparing _____ and _____

from _____ (book title(s))

How alike?

☐ _____

_____

_____

_____

☐ _____

_____

_____

_____

_____

Support from text or texts

☐ _____

_____

_____

_____

☐ _____

_____

_____

How different?

☐ _____

_____

_____

☐ _____

_____

_____

Support from text or texts

☐ _____

_____

_____

☐ _____

_____

_____

Supporting Similarities

Select two items to compare. In each box labeled Similar, write one point of comparison, and in each box labeled Different, write one point of contrast. Then, in the Support column, write the evidence from the text that supports the similarities or differences.

Book title(s)

Item 1 _____ Item 2

_____

Support

❏ _____

_____

_____

_____

❏ _____

_____

_____

_____

★ _____

_____

_____

_____

★ _____

_____

_____

_____

Similar

Similar

Different

Different

Support

❏ _____

_____

_____

_____

❏ _____

_____

_____

_____

★ _____

_____

_____

_____

★ _____

_____

_____

_____

Which similarity or difference do you feel is most important in this story? Explain.

_____

_____

Summary

Skill: *Synthesize and restate the key points from the text in a sentence or short paragraph.*

About Summary

Giving a summary—a concise recap of main points—may sound simple, but it is a complex skill. To summarize effectively, students must distinguish between ideas that the author deems important and those that are interesting but secondary. Students must also be able to differentiate between main ideas and details.

Why Is This Skill Important?

Summarizing can help students monitor their own comprehension (*Can I recap in my own words what I just read?*), remember information, and think about the text as a whole.

GETTING STARTED

Model Lesson: Writing chapter summaries with *Sadako and the Thousand Paper Cranes* by Eleanor Coerr (Puffin Books, 1977)

✳ **Read aloud from the book's opening chapters.** I model summarizing by reading aloud the first two chapters of *Sadako and the Thousand Paper Cranes*. This is the story of Sadako, an 11-year-old girl who develops leukemia as a result of radiation caused by an atomic bomb, which was dropped over Hiroshima, Japan. The opening chapters set the scene: Sadako and her family join the Peace Day celebration in which the dead are honored. While reading, I ask the class to pay special attention to the main characters, setting, problem, and important events.

✳ **Help students focus on the story's important points.** I record the following ideas on the Puzzling graphic organizer (page 94). Using as few words as I can, I write down the important points for each category. Later, we'll decide which ideas best summarize the story and put them into categories.

> Setting: Japan—August, 1954
>
> Big event: Peace Day "celebration"—happens every year.
>
> Character: Sadako Sasaki—main character. She runs fast. Sadako looks forward to celebration—fun with friends. Sadako enjoys celebration.
>
> Character: Mr. Sasaki—reminded of how awful bombing was. Mr. Sasaki lost six members of his family in the bombing.
>
> Problem: Sadako sees the celebration as a carnival, while Mr. and Mrs. Sasaki consider it a time to pay respect to those who were killed by the bomb dropped on Hiroshima.

* **Eliminate unnecessary ideas and write a structured summary.** I explain that now we have to evaluate each idea and trim down the list by eliminating unnecessary ideas and combining others. I remind students that we are eliminating some ideas that may be interesting but are probably not essential to the outcome of the story. We work to make our ideas fit into this format: _____(main character) wants _____ (character desire) but _____ (problem), so _____ (solution). *Sadako wants to have fun at the Peace Day celebration but her father has bad memories of the destruction caused by the bomb dropped on Hiroshima, so they act in different ways.*

* **Help students combine key ideas.** With more advanced students, I think aloud while combining ideas: "In one sentence, I can explain what Peace Day is and why it is celebrated. In another sentence, I can use phrases and conjunctions (*and, but*) to put together several ideas: who Sadako is, what she likes to do, and how her father and she react differently." I model this on a copy of the Combine and Condense graphic organizer (page 95) and end up with the following summary: *There is a Peace Day "celebration" every year to remember those who*

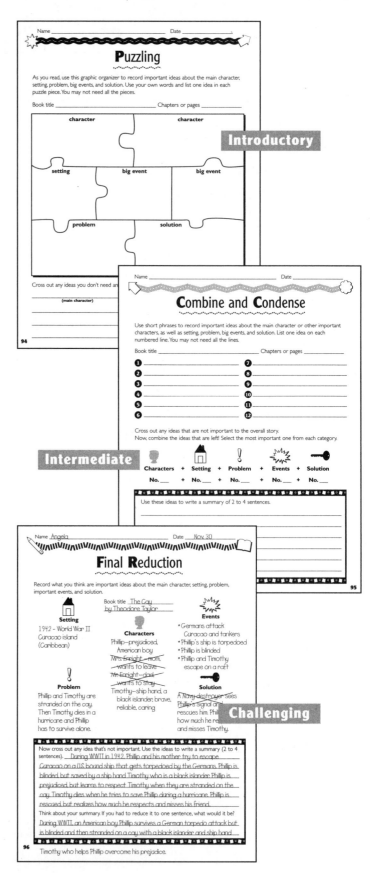

died when a bomb was dropped on Hiroshima. Sadako Sasaki, the main character, always enjoys the celebration with her friends, but her father, who lost six family members in the bombing, is reminded of how awful that day was.

✳ **Show students how to further synthesize these ideas.** For students who will use the Final Reduction organizer (page 96), I explain how I could take this summary and reduce it to one main-idea sentence: *Every year Sadako and her family go to the Peace Day celebration, where people commemorate in different ways the lives of victims of the Hiroshima bombing.*

✳ **When students are able to distinguish between "important" main ideas and "interesting" details, they should be ready to complete the basic tiered activity.** Observing students' responses during lessons will help determine when they're ready for the other activities. Throughout my teaching, I emphasize that there is no one right way to create a summary, but that the purpose is to reduce the text to just the key points. In order to improve their summarization skills, most students will probably need repeated modeling of this process as well as examples of strong and weak summaries, followed by critiques and discussions.

USING TIERED ACTIVITIES

Readers will:

❋ Record all ideas that may be important about character, setting, events, problem, and solution. [All]

❋ Evaluate the importance of each idea to the outcome of the story. [All]

❋ Eliminate ideas that are interesting but only secondarily important to the outcome of the story. [All]

❋ Write a brief summary that contains only key points. [All]

❋ Condense and combine ideas. [Intermediate and Challenging]

❋ Reduce the essential ideas to one sentence. [Challenging]

Graphic Organizers:

Introductory Level: Puzzling (page 94)

Tip: Remind students that when they are selecting key ideas, they are determining what the author would see as important to the overall story.

Intermediate Level: Combine and Condense (page 95)

Challenging Level: Final Reduction (page 96)

Books Worth Using:

Hiroshima by Laurence Yep (Scholastic, 1995)

The True Confessions of Charlotte Doyle by Avi (Avon Flare Books, 1990)

Pink and Say by Patricia Polacco (Philomel,1994) *Picture book*

Puzzling

As you read, use this graphic organizer to record important ideas about the main character, setting, problem, big events, and solution. Use your own words and list one idea in each puzzle piece. You may not need all the pieces.

Book title _____ Chapters or pages _____

character

character

setting

big event

big event

problem

solution

Cross out any ideas you don't need and use the ideas you have left to write a short summary.

_____ **wants** _____
(main character)

_____ **but** _____

_____ **, so** _____

_____ .

Name _____ Date _____

Combine and Condense

Use short phrases to record important ideas about the main character or other important characters, as well as setting, problem, big events, and solution. List one idea on each numbered line. You may not need all the lines.

Book title _____ Chapters or pages _____

1 _____   **7** _____

2 _____   **8** _____

3 _____   **9** _____

4 _____   **10** _____

5 _____   **11** _____

6 _____   **12** _____

Cross out any ideas that are not important to the overall story.
Now, combine the ideas that are left! Select the most important one from each category.

Characters	+	**Setting**	+	**Problem**	+	**Events**	+	**Solution**
No. ___	+	**No.** ___	+	**No.** ___	+	**No.** ___	+	**No.** ___

Use these ideas to write a summary of 2 to 4 sentences.

_____

_____

_____

_____

_____

_____

Final **R**eduction

Record what you think are important ideas about the main character, setting, problem, important events, and solution.

Setting

Book title _____
_____

Characters

Events

Problem

Solution

Now cross out any idea that's not important. Use the ideas to write a summary (2 to 4 sentences). _____
_____
_____
_____
_____
_____

Think about your summary. If you had to reduce it to one sentence, what would it be?
_____
_____

Main Idea

Skill: *Create a summary statement of key, implicit ideas from a passage.*

About Main Idea

When readers seek out the main idea(s) of a passage, their job is to briefly summarize the implicit elements to get the big idea(s) in the writing. This lesson asks students to phrase the main idea in a sentence that goes beyond a summary statement—to show the deeper meaning behind events and actions.

Why Is This Skill Important?

It's difficult, and usually not necessary, for readers to remember everything they read; they can focus by culling meaning from important events and information and focusing on main ideas.

GETTING STARTED

Model Lesson: Identifying main ideas with *Nettie's Trip South* by Ann Turner (Simon & Schuster, 1987)

Identifying the main idea of a story is a difficult skill for many students to master, and it's even more difficult when students work with authentic literature in which there are usually several key ideas woven together.

✳ **Initiate main idea instruction by using a short passage or a picture book that has a clear message,** like *Nettie's Trip South.* This powerful picture book is based on a diary that was kept by the author's great-grandmother. It's a letter that Nettie, a ten-year-old girl from Albany, New York, writes to her cousin Addie just before the Civil War. In it she describes the disturbing realities of slavery, as witnessed firsthand during her trip to Richmond, Virginia. Nettie writes that the sight of slaves living in poverty on a wealthy plantation haunt her, and that bearing witness to the Negro Auction made her physically sick. She comments, "If we slipped into a black skin like a tight coat, everything would change."

✳ **Think out loud about how to generate the main idea.** I explain that I'm going to describe, in one sentence, the big idea or the central meaning behind the book. I take note of the title and talk about why I think the author used this title and what it has to do with the important message of the book. (For example, the economy of the South in this time period is driven by agriculture and slavery. Nettie's trip involves a learning experience about the realities of slavery.) Next, I invite students to help me list on the board

or overhead some of the important events (or details) in the book. After the list is complete, I provide a main idea statement that pulls this information together: "I think the main idea is that Nettie is upset by the white southerners' treatment of pre–Civil War slaves, who suffered many injustices because of the color of their skin." Then I go back through our list and the book, showing how the events, details, and title clues support this main idea.

* **Using the key ideas in the book, brainstorm alternative titles that can help students generate a main idea statement.** For example, I suggest the book could be called *Nettie's Nightmare* because the experiences depicted in the book continued to haunt her when she returned home.

* **When students can provide a main idea statement for a text, match them with the appropriate tiered activities.** Students who are more advanced in this area will be able to move from the main idea to a more concise statement of theme.

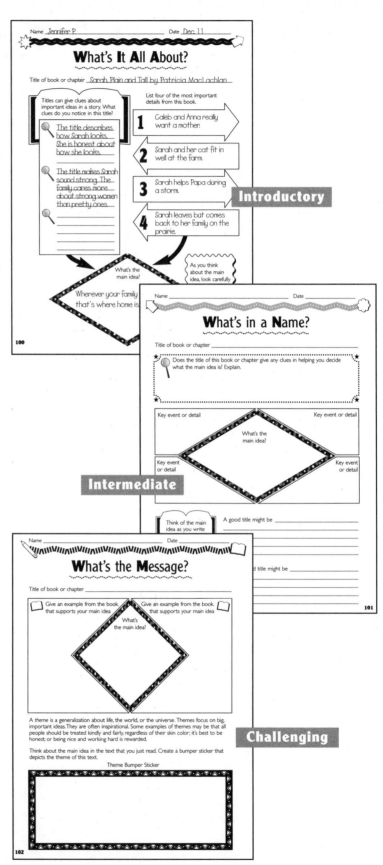

USING TIERED ACTIVITIES

Readers will:

❀ Explain whether or not the main idea of the book is reflected in the title. [Introductory and Intermediate]

❀ List important details from the passage. [Introductory]

❀ Determine the main idea. [All]

❀ Create new titles for the book based on key ideas from the book and provide a rationale for each new title. [Intermediate]

❀ Transform the main idea from an interpretation into a theme. [Challenging]

❀ Design a bumper sticker that depicts the book's theme. [Challenging]

Graphic Organizers:

Introductory Level: What's It All About? (page 100)

Tip: Provide students with instruction and practice in summarization (see page 91) to help them identify key events that they can use as details in the organizer.

Intermediate Level: What's in a Name? (page 101)

Challenging Level: What's the Message? (page 102)

Tip: Students need to understand the concept of theme to complete the bumper sticker on this activity page. Make sure to discuss main idea in terms of theme. Themes are generalizations that state big, important ideas, and are often inspirational and more condensed than the summary-style statement students have been working with. I begin by sharing themes from stories they know. For example, in the popular picture book *Ira Sleeps Over* (Waber, 1972), a theme might be "Be your own person." Some additional examples are provided in the What's the Message? organizer.

Books Worth Using:

The Cricket in Times Square by George Selden (Farrar, Strauss & Giroux, 1960)

My Brother Sam Is Dead by James Lincoln Collier (Scholastic, 1974)

Faithful Elephants, A True Story of Animals, People and War by Yukio Tsuchiya (Houghton Mifflin, 1988) *Picture book*

Name _____ Date _____

What's It All About?

Title of book or chapter _____

Titles can give clues about important ideas in a story. What clues do you notice in this title?

_____
_____
_____
_____
_____
_____
_____
_____
_____
_____

List four of the most important details from this book.

1

2

3

4

What's the main idea?

As you think about the main idea, look carefully at the clues from the title and the details you listed. What's important? What is your list mostly about?

What's in a Name?

Title of book or chapter _____

 Does the title of this book or chapter give any clues in helping you decide what the main idea is? Explain.

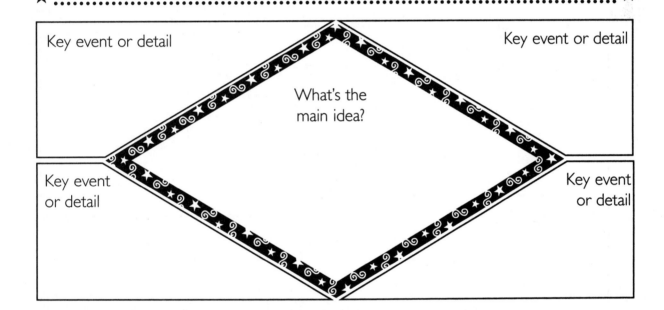

Key event or detail

Key event or detail

What's the main idea?

Key event or detail

Key event or detail

Think of the main idea as you write a new title for this text.

A good title might be _____

_____

because _____

_____

_____

Think of a second main idea as you write another new title for this text.

Another good title might be _____

_____

because _____

_____

_____

Name _____ Date _____

What's the Message?

Title of book or chapter _____

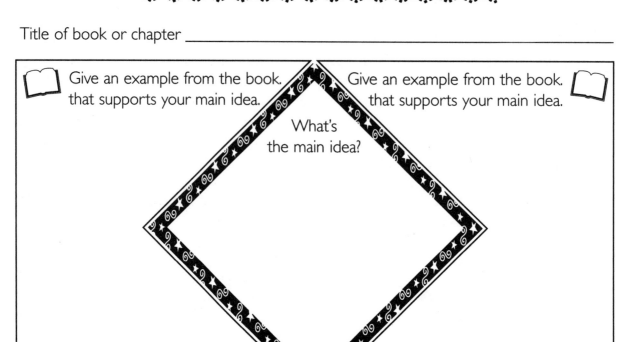

Give an example from the book. that supports your main idea.

Give an example from the book. that supports your main idea.

What's the main idea?

A *theme* is a generalization about life, the world, or the universe. Themes focus on big, important ideas. They are often inspirational. Some examples of themes may be that all people should be treated kindly and fairly, regardless of their skin color; it's best to be honest; or being nice and working hard is rewarded.

Think about the main idea in the text that you just read. Create a bumper sticker that depicts the theme of this text.

Theme Bumper Sticker

Figurative Language

Skill: *Identify a simile or metaphor and explain the author's meaning.*

About Figurative Language

Figurative language employs images and comparisons to create a special feeling or effect. Similes and metaphors are two of the most commonly used figures of speech. A simile compares two unlike things using the words *like* or *as* (*She was shaking like a leaf*). A metaphor compares two unlike things implicitly (*That problem is a thorn in my side*).

Why Is This Skill Important?

To understand figurative language, students must "see beyond" the literal meaning of the words so they read the text at a deeper level.

GETTING STARTED

Model Lesson: Interpreting figurative language with "No Difference" from *Where the Sidewalk Ends* by Shel Silverstein (Harper & Row, 1974), "Magic Carpet" from *A Light in the Attic* by Shel Silverstein (Harper & Row, 1981), and *Encounter* by Jane Yolen (Voyager Books/Harcourt Brace, 1992)

* **Provide an explanation of simile and metaphor by introducing clear examples from well-liked poetry.** Using Shel Silverstein's poem "No Difference," we analyze the

phrases he uses to tell us that we are all the same in the dark: "small as a peanut, big as a giant, rich as a sultan, and poor as mite." We discuss how these similes create much more colorful images than plainly saying we are all the same inside, despite our differences physically, socially, economically, and so on.

Once students understand similes, I move on to metaphors. In "Magic Carpet," the poet implicitly compares the imagination to a magic carpet: "You have a magic carpet / That will whiz you through the air / To Spain or Maine or Africa / If you just tell it where. . . ." The question *What could that magic carpet be?* helps students who are reading the poem literally, and helps them understand Silverstein's message: that they have the option to use or not use their imaginations.

* **Provide some practice identifying similes and metaphors.** Similes are usually less confusing than metaphors because they are less abstract, and they have the signal word *as* or *like* in the text. To help students learn how to distinguish between metaphors or similes, I use paired simile and metaphor examples like the following

in a focus lesson. We discuss how the use of similes and metaphors creates different images.

• The growing boy was as tall as a tree.
  The mighty redwood stand of football players raised their helmets to the crowd.

• Annie's room is like the Wild West—anything goes.
  Down the hall is a dump with rotten apples and dirty gym socks: my sister's room.

• The dog ran like the wind to warn us of the fire.
  A four-siren alarm, the dog barked and howled until we woke up.

✳ **Support students as they interpret similes and metaphors in longer passages.** I follow up with model passages from *Encounter*. This book uses a Taino boy's perspective to tell of the landing of the strange, greedy white men (Columbus and his crew) on San Salvador. We discuss the following lines and I assess their interpretations to see if they are ready to work with metaphors and similes independently. (Note: no page numbers are given.)

• I watched their chief smile.
  It was the serpent's smile—no lips and all teeth. (metaphor)

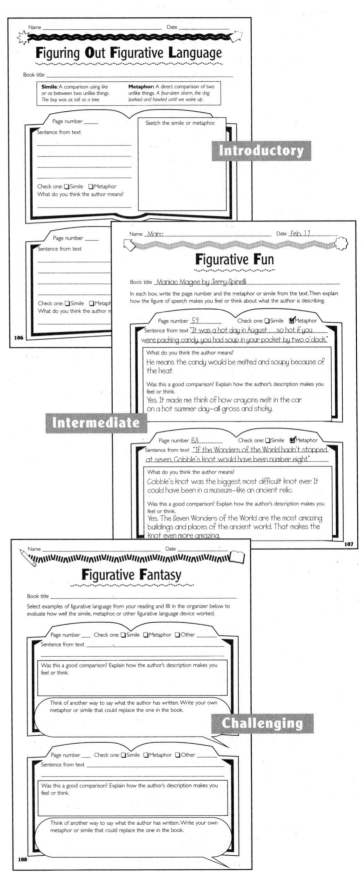

104

- They [the chief's eyes] were blue and gray like the shifting sea. (simile)

- But in my dream that night, three great-winged birds with voices like thunder rode wild waves in our bay. (simile)

- And many of them had hair growing like bushes on their chins. (simile)

- The hand felt like flesh and blood, but the skin was moon to my sun. (simile and metaphor)

✳ **When students can identify a simile and a metaphor and distinguish between the two, match them with the appropriate tiered activities.** Students who are more advanced in this area might try identifying other types of figurative language, such as personification, through which an author attributes human characteristics or actions to nonhuman things (*The sun winked at me*).

USING TIERED ACTIVITIES

Readers will:

❋ Identify a sentence or phrase as a simile or metaphor, and explain its meaning in the text. [All]

❋ Clarify the image or special effect created. [Intermediate]

❋ Explain how a metaphorical image influences their feelings about the topic. [Intermediate and Challenging]

❋ Create a figure of speech that is similar to the one in the text. [Challenging]

Graphic Organizers:

Introductory Level: Figuring Out Figurative Language (page 106)

Tip: You may want to assign a passage, poem, or chapter that contains several good examples of similes or metaphors. With practice, your students should be able to do an independent "free search" or a "collection" while reading.

Intermediate Level: Figurative Fun (page 107)

Challenging Level: Figurative Fantasy (page 108)

Books Worth Using:

Yellow Bird and Me by Joyce Hansen (Clarion Books, 1986)

The Midnight Horse by Sid Fleischman (William Morrow & Co., 1990)

Encounter by Jane Yolen (Harcourt, Brace & Co., 1992) *Picture book*

Figuring Out Figurative Language

Book title _____

Simile: A comparison using *like* or *as* between two unlike things. *The boy was as tall as a tree.*

Metaphor: A direct comparison of two unlike things. *A four-siren alarm, the dog barked and howled until we woke up.*

Page number _____

Sentence from text

_____

_____

_____

_____

Check one: ☐ Simile ☐ Metaphor
What do you think the author means?

_____

Sketch the simile or metaphor.

Page number _____

Sentence from text

_____

_____

_____

_____

Check one: ☐ Simile ☐ Metaphor
What do you think the author means?

_____

Sketch the simile or metaphor.

Name _____ Date _____

Figurative Fun

Book title _____

In each box, write the page number and the metaphor or simile from the text. Then explain how the figure of speech makes you feel or think about what the author is describing.

Page number _____   Check one: ☐ Simile ☐ Metaphor

Sentence from text _____

_____

What do you think the author means?

Was this a good comparison? Explain how the author's description makes you feel or think.

Page number _____   Check one: ☐ Simile ☐ Metaphor

Sentence from text _____

_____

What do you think the author means?

Was this a good comparison? Explain how the author's description makes you feel or think.

Name _____   Date _____

Figurative Fantasy

Book title _____

Select examples of figurative language from your reading and fill in the organizer below to evaluate how well the simile, metaphor, or other figurative language device worked.

Page number ___   Check one: ☐ Simile ☐ Metaphor ☐ Other _____

Sentence from text _____

_____

Was this a good comparison? Explain how the author's description makes you feel or think.

Think of another way to say what the author has written. Write your own metaphor or simile that could replace the one in the book.

Page number ___   Check one: ☐ Simile ☐ Metaphor ☐ Other _____

Sentence from text _____

_____

Was this a good comparison? Explain how the author's description makes you feel or think.

Think of another way to say what the author has written. Write your own metaphor or simile that could replace the one in the book.

Journal Responses

Skill: *In a journal entry, respond to literature thoughtfully and use supporting information from the text.*

About Journal Responses

A journal response is not meant to go beyond a first draft. The content is considered more important than the mechanics. Journals allow students to focus on their interpretations of specific elements of the story. The response is as writing should be: thinking and feeling written down.

Why Is This Skill Important?

Journal writing enables students to organize and articulate their thoughts. As we know, reading reinforces writing, and writing reinforces reading. In addition, like oral responses, journals allow each student to express his or her understanding of the reading, but may encourage more in-depth, personal responses.

GETTING STARTED ⇨

✳ **Make sure students have a journal or notebook that they can use exclusively for writing responses to literature.** This will become their reading journal, reading response notebook, or whatever you choose to call it.

✳ **Model using the journal as a place to collect ideas about your reading that help you better understand a story or text.** Encourage students to date their entries so that they can refer back to previous entries and check their earlier reflections and understandings. This process will help students move forward with their thinking.

✳ **Review different skills and strategies that students can use each time they respond to literature.** Look back through the lessons in this book—any skill lesson or activity page may serve as a springboard for a journal response. I allow students to write in all types of ways in their journals, including free writing, writing in response to a question or prompt, filling in a diagram or chart, and sketching.

✳ **Differentiate instruction through the activities you design or the level of questions that you pose.** Some types of responses require more critical thinking than others. For example, asking students to compare and contrast events is generally more involved than asking them to describe an event. In the table on page 111 I've provided examples of questions that represent introductory, intermediate, and

challenging levels of comprehension and interpretation.

* **Model any type of response you want students to be able to make in their journals.** I provide examples of strong and weak journal entries for any skill we've worked on. For example, if a student is writing about character traits and responds, "I like this character because he's funny," I comment that I'm not convinced about this until the reader gives me some evidence to support why he thinks that character is funny. We refer back to the activity pages we've completed for character analysis to review ways to respond with support from the text. I encourage students to use the activity pages they've used and are comfortable with as a template for their journal responses.

USING TIERED ACTIVITIES

Readers will:

* Identify components of the story. [All]

* Support their responses with information from the text and from their own experiences. [All]

* Make judgments based on information from the text and from their own experiences. [Intermediate]

* Analyze story elements and create alternate scenarios. [Challenging]

Journal Response Activities

Since students will respond to these tiered prompts in their individual journals, no reproducible activity pages are included. Students should read to a designated place in the text and then respond to the appropriate prompt or model their response after one of the activity pages they've already completed.

Sample Journal Response Prompts

	〰️ Introductory 〰️	∿ Intermediate ∿	⑊ Challenging ⑊
CHARACTER ANALYSIS	Which is your favorite character? Explain why this is your favorite character. How are you similar to and different from this character?	List 3–5 traits that describe your favorite character. Explain why she or he is your favorite character. Which traits do you admire or like the most? Which traits do you not like? Why?	Contrast your favorite character with your least favorite character. Explain why you chose these two characters.
STORY MAPS	What do you think is the most important event in the story? Explain why this is the most important one.	Describe the most important event. Explain why you think this is the most important event. (How did it affect the characters and their actions?)	Summarize the most important event. Explain how you would change it to give the story a different twist.
SETTING	Tell where and when this story takes place.	Tell where and when this story takes place. (If there is more than one setting, briefly describe each of them.) Why do you think the author chose this setting (or these settings) for this book?	If this story happened some-where else or at another time, how would the plot be different?
CAUSE AND EFFECT	List three actions (causes) and three resulting effects.	Describe an important cause-effect relationship from this story and come up with a different (but plausible) effect for the cause. Why do you think the author chose the original sequence of events?	Pick a critical cause-and-effect relationship and explain how a different cause or effect might have changed the whole story.
SUMMARY	Brainstorm ideas relating to the 5 W's about this book: Who (characters), when and where (setting), what (what happens), and why (why is this story happening—what's the problem that needs to be solved?). Highlight or circle the most important ideas.	Complete a story map and write a summary of the story using the information from your map.	Imagine that you are writing a telegram to a friend about this book and you are paying by the word! Write a brief summary of the book with the most important points in one sentence.

Professional Works Cited

Lane, B. (1993). *After the end: Teaching and learning creative revision.* Portsmouth, NH: Heinemann.

Swartz, R.J., & Parks, S. (1994). *Infusing critical and creative thinking into content instruction: A lesson design handbook for the elementary grades.* Pacific Grove, CA: Critical Thinking Press and Software.

Tomlinson, C.A. (1999). *The Differentiated classroom: Responding to the needs of all learners.* Alexandria, VA: ASCD.

Vacca, R.T., & Vacca, J.L. (1993). *Content area reading.* 4th ed. New York: HarperCollins.